'Powerful, challenging and encouraging. unpacks the rich teaching of 1 Corinthia to our context. Be inspired to play your p... Evangelical Alliance

'I've been privileged in my life to meet some truly inspiring people – and Andy is one of them. His passion and faith challenge you to be more and do more for Christ, and he leads by example. To Andy, the big challenges we come up against in life are just opportunities for God to show up and show off, and in this book you'll get a glimpse of what makes a legend like this tick. Read it and be inspired.' – **Revd. Paul Lloyd**, Victory Outreach Manchester

'Andy Hawthorne has an extraordinary track record of ministry among some of the most deprived and vulnerable young people in our society. The Message Trust has brought the love of Jesus Christ to many thousands searching for the meaning of life. I commend him to you wholeheartedly.' – **Revd. Nicky Gumbel**, Holy Trinity Brompton

'*A Burning Heart* is a must read, and a timely read, for all who are working to impact the cities of our broken world. Andy's insight into Paul's letter to the church at Corinth reveals that we are faced with many of the same challenges that the early church had. Get your highlighter ready, the book is packed with take-aways on how to present the timeless message of the love of Jesus Christ.' – **David Koop (Dmin)**, Coastal Church (Vancouver)

'Andy Hawthorne's faith in Jesus is inspirational. It's a faith that always leads to action and it shines from this book.' – **Tim Vine**, Comedian

A BURNING HEART

A

BURNING

HEART

ANDY HAWTHORNE

First published in Great Britain in 2022 by The Message Trust
Lancaster House, Harper Road, Manchester, M22 4RG, UK

ISBN 978-1-9163489-6-7

Cover design and typesetting: Hannah Beatrice Owens
Cover photograph: Gary Saldana/Unsplash
Internal photography: Laura Vinck/Unsplash, Rachael Silvester,
Hannah Beatrice Owens, Ruth Teague

CONTENTS

ACKNOWLEDGEMENTS

A Burning Heart was originally delivered over around twelve months as I taught week in and week out from the beautiful letter to the Corinthians for our growing Message Trust team.

Thanks to our Message Creative department and especially once again to Al Metcalfe who took that material and turned it into the book you now have in your hands.

Once again though I'd like to dedicate this book to Michele. In 1983 she said 'I do' and little did she know what a rollercoaster of breakthroughs and heartbreaks she would be buying into. Through it all though, she has never wavered in her passion for Jesus and love for her husband, and I love her right back.

YOUR BEST YEAR EVER

None of us will quickly forget 2020 and the impact that Covid had on each of our lives. As we approached Christmas that year there was lots of uncertainty. What would the rules be? Would we be able to see friends and family? And (for many who'd been hit by the financial impact of the pandemic): how will we afford Christmas? With questions abounding, and wanting people to know they weren't alone, the entire Message staff downed tools and went out delivering gift hampers on to the estates around our headquarters in South Manchester. We gave away over 900 Christmas hampers, and Message teams around the UK delivered thousands more.

The results were incredible. Even more precious than the looks on people's faces when they received these unexpected gifts were the stories we later heard of many of these same people receiving Christ. But even before we loaded up the truck that day, we'd seen the favour of God on our plans.

We'd decided our hampers weren't going to be any old ordinary hampers. We weren't going to go for Tesco value hampers or Aldi hampers. We were going to go for Waitrose hampers. We wanted those for whom life was really tough, to have the best. So my son Sam, who is involved in running our Community Grocery ministry, went to buy a vast quantity of stuff from Waitrose and then literally had to scan through every item, thousands of them, at the till. It took him an hour and a half, and he ran up a huge bill. Can you imagine being the person in the queue behind him that day?

But as he was at the till, putting all these items through, an amazing thing happened. The manager kept coming up telling him that offers were coming on the prices, one after another: 'Oh an offer's just come on all veg – it's just gone down to 20p!' And we bought a lot of veg! Sam said it was like the TV show Pointless, watching the amount that it was costing us going down and down!

If Sam had gone half an hour earlier, he would have missed it. But in God's timing and by God's kindness, we saved thousands of pounds. You might be thinking, 'Andy, it was just a coincidence. You just happened to turn up at the right time when the Christmas discounts kicked in.' But you know what? I've learned that the closer I get to the centre of God's will, the more 'coincidences' I seem to see. I've learned that God cares about every detail of my life. And more than anything, I want to live under his favour.

Paul's first letter to the Corinthians is 16 chapters of pure heavenly wisdom. It's a must-read, I believe, for anyone, anywhere, who wants to live under the favour of God. Now, I'm definitely not saying that if we obey the book of 1 Corinthians, our weekly shop's suddenly going to be a lot cheaper. What I am saying is that if we do God's work God's way – if we focus on the poor, keep Jesus central, love his Word and take it seriously – I believe our life will be defined much more by heavenly intervention. I've experienced that throughout my life. The more I focus on the things that count, the more I experience the miraculous in the everyday.

Don't you want to live that kind of life? It's the best life possible, especially at a time in history like this when so many people are confused, so many don't know where to turn. We need to look at God's Word, like 1 Corinthians, and discover a vision of the life he has planned for us – a life of experiencing the glory, the breakthrough, the kingdom to come, but also the power to overcome the worst that life throws at us now. That's the Christian life.

I believe God wants you to have your best year yet. It may not necessarily be your easiest year yet, but your best year yet. God operates in the realm of people who are faithful with small things. He allows them to be faithful with much. God's got your best year yet for you if you can just keep your eyes on Jesus and be faithful at a time like this.

As I've dug deeper into the themes in the letter and the context that it was written into, I've realised again and again how utterly relevant it is for the world we're living in and the days we're experiencing here in Manchester and around the world.

Corinth was a cosmopolitan city and famously debauched. To think of Corinth then, think of Magaluf today, think of Vegas, think of a dodgy, immoral city. At the centre of Corinth was a vast temple with a thousand temple prostitutes and much of the religion was based around debauched sexual activity. The Greeks even had a word 'Corinthizean', which meant to live like a Corinthian. It meant to be depraved, to be a sensual, anything-goes kind of person.

It was into that context Paul planted a church. J. C. Pollock wrote this: 'Corinth was the biggest city Paul had yet encountered, a brash new commercial metropolis... It squeezed nearly a quarter of a million people into a comparatively small area, a large proportion being slaves engaged in the unending movement of goods. Slaves or free, Corinthians were rootless, cut off from their country background, drawn from races and districts all over the empire...

a curiously close parallel to the population of a 20th century "inner-city."'

And in many, many ways that's the kind of context we're operating in as The Message. This ancient book speaks into our modern context for mission and what we want to achieve.

It's clear that despite seeing remarkable fruit in his ministry, Paul was thrown at first. You can imagine him turning up in Corinth wondering, 'What the heck?!' as he arrived. He describes in 1 Corinthians 2:3 being 'full of much fear and trembling' as he contemplated planting a church in this context. And yet he learned that the love of Christ could take root in any culture, anywhere, no matter how anti-God it appears. No matter how much the culture is against the gospel, we can see God break in and bring transformation. When Paul left Corinth after 18 months, I'm sure he left thinking, 'If it can take root here, it can take root anywhere.'

And it seems to me that Paul did it in the hardest possible way: he started by focusing on the synagogue in Corinth. He taught about the gospel of free grace, about Jesus being the only way to the Father. Initially it was received wonderfully as the synagogue leader came to Christ. Imagine how exciting that was for Paul. But soon enough, opposition came and he got booted out of the synagogue. I love what Paul did next – he planted a church in the house next door, the very next building along! In this crazy culture, bombarded by secularism, Paul just plants this beautiful church. And in Acts 18 it says that in that church in that house next to the synagogue, many believed and were baptised.

Wouldn't you have loved to have seen that move of the Spirit in Corinth? Paul must have left so encouraged and excited. He must have left a little bit of his heart behind. Sometimes I've experienced that myself, when I've done a week of schools missions or I've been away for a weekend with a church doing a mission. Seeing people and God doing great stuff, I'll leave a little bit of my heart with them. How much more must Paul have felt that after 18 months in Corinth?

And so it's no wonder he writes so strongly and so passionately to the Christians in 1 Corinthians. The reason for writing this letter is, we find out, because pretty soon after he left, strange and slightly dodgy teaching started filtering into the church and began to divide it. And rather than being the fiery, world-changing, non-conforming church Paul had planted, they started to compromise, to become a bit wishy-washy, and to take on the priorities of the world.

So 1 Corinthians, I guess, is primarily a call to live as God's people in an overwhelmingly non-Christian culture. Again, so relevant for us today when we can see culture moving away from the Word of God. We need people who can stand strong and firm.

Did you know in our Parliament buildings there's a mosaic with the words from Psalm 127:1 on it: 'Unless the Lord builds the house, the labourers labour in vain.' Wow! The whole of the Houses of Parliament, the whole of our political system, the whole of our structures in this funny little nation called the United Kingdom are built around those mighty words. And they are as true today as when they were written. They're as true today as when those Parliament buildings were built, when those great men decided they wanted that verse to be foundational for everything those Houses were about.

Did you know that our late Queen Elizabeth II was given a Bible at her coronation, and the Archbishop of Canterbury knelt down and said, 'Our gracious Queen... we present you with this Book, the most valuable thing that this world affords'? Everything that's good about our country, everything that's good about our constitution is built upon it: 'Unless the Lord builds the house, the labourers labour in vain.' Unless we build our lives on the living Word of God, the most precious thing this life affords, how can we expect to thrive?

When the UK government announced the third Covid lockdown at the beginning of 2021, one thing that had changed was that worshipping in churches was one of the things it was now acceptable to leave home for. That was a big shift from March the year before, when all the churches were closed. Maybe our leaders had realised that our nation needed the church at a time like this like never before. I believe it. We need the church to do all the beautiful things we've always done, and more than ever. Serving our communities, feeding the poor, praying for our neighbourhoods. Loving people who are struggling, filling the gaps.

And we need the Word of God to 'build the house.' We'll only grow stronger as a nation with the Word of God at the centre. I can't tell people how to live, but the Bible can. My job is not to say, 'Oh, you naughty person – sort your life out!' I'm saying, 'God said this for your good because he loves you.'

If we're going to thrive and be fruitful, we need to build our lives on the living Word of God. We can't afford to compromise to the culture. We can't be people who are walking down a road that's leading to destruction. We're countercultural – we're the salmon swimming against the tide doing beautiful things in Jesus' name.

Let's allow the Lord to build things in us and through us as we do his work his way. Let's keep his living Word front and centre. It's the way this coming year is going to be your best year yet.

....

A PRAYER

Lord, we look to you at a time like this. We thank
you that you've not finished with us yet, but ask that
this year will be our best, most fruitful year yet.

We pray your church will rise up and love people radically.
We pray that expectancy, passion and surrender will mark
our lives like never before, and in it all, you will be glorified.

Amen.

....

1 CORINTHIANS 1:1-9

LIVING UP TO WHO YOU ARE

Paul, called to be an apostle of Christ Jesus by the will of God, and our brother Sosthenes,

To the church of God in Corinth, to those sanctified in Christ Jesus and called to be his holy people, together with all those everywhere who call on the name of our Lord Jesus Christ – their Lord and ours:

Grace and peace to you from God our Father and the Lord Jesus Christ.

I always thank my God for you because of his grace given you in Christ Jesus. For in him you have been enriched in every way – with all kinds of speech and with all knowledge – God thus confirming our testimony about Christ among you. Therefore you do not lack any spiritual gift as you eagerly wait for our Lord Jesus Christ to be revealed. He will also keep you firm to the end, so that you will be blameless on the day of our Lord Jesus Christ. God is faithful, who has called you into fellowship with his Son, Jesus Christ our Lord.

Paul had planted a church in a pagan, sex-obsessed society called Corinth, and he'd seen a lot of fruit. He'd seen Acts 6 and 7 stuff – a huge increase in disciples, large numbers coming to be obedient to the faith. For 18 months it seemed like he was riding a wave – it was one of the most fruitful, significant times of Paul's ministry. But when he went off on his next ministry journey, things started to go a bit weird in Corinth. Paul heard stories of divisions and plain sinfulness in the church. So he writes a letter, which we now know as 1 Corinthians.

It starts the way ancient letters always used to start by letting you know who's written it and who it's written to. In ancient times they didn't write 'Dear John' at the start and 'Love, Bill' at the end. They used to put it all up at the top. So he writes, 'Paul called by an apostle of Christ Jesus by the will of God and our brother Sosthenes. To the church of God in Corinth...'

Spot this first of all: Paul never forgot throughout his whole ministry who he was. He was called by Jesus. There was a high calling on his life and it defined everything he did and everything he said. It led him into incredible sacrifice and suffering, but he came out in a blaze of glory.

But it wasn't just Paul who wrote this letter, it was 'our brother Sosthenes.' Sosthenes was probably the synagogue leader who was beaten up in Acts 18. It must have been slightly annoying for Sosthenes. He's the co-writer, but nobody ever talks about Sosthenes' letter to the Corinthians! I guess he had to learn what lots of us have to learn: to just allow others to take the credit. It doesn't really matter. We just serve faithfully like Sosthenes.

Then, before he launches into his letter (which as we'll see over the coming chapters, deals with all kinds of challenging behaviour around divisions and downright disobedience), he tells the Corinthian church how amazing they are.

I've learned a little leadership secret for dealing with difficult situations when behaviour has to be challenged. No leader likes doing it, but it must be done from time to time. If I'm challenging things that I know aren't right about a person, the first thing I want to do is share what's good about that person. Before I launch in saying, 'You really need to sort this out', I always want to start by telling them who they are in God. I want to find the goodness, find where the Holy Spirit's at work in them. (I've given away my secret there. If you ever get called into my office and I start to tell you how great you are and how the Holy Spirit's on your life, get worried!)

Anyway, Paul does exactly that here in the book of 1 Corinthians. Before launching in, he reminds them who they are and challenges them to live up to it. The key, I believe, to any positive change of behaviour will always be found there.

The first reason, in verse 1, is that they were a called people. Paul knew he was called, and he wanted to remind them they were called. We each had a personal invitation from the living God the day we got saved. We had a personal invitation to be part of his church, his bride, his family. God personally invited us to good works planned in advance for us to do, and the great joy of life is fulfilling those good works. You're a called person and when you realise truly that God called you out of darkness into his wonderful light, how can you live the same?

The second thing that Paul says is they were a sanctified people. He actually says, verse 2, 'you've been sanctified in every way'. The day you were called and the day you accepted that call, a work started in your life. You were called from one degree of glory to another. You're meant to be moving forward. I've often said that a Christian is somebody who can say, 'I'm not what I should be, but I'm not what I was, and it's all because of Jesus.'

We're on a journey – and never forget, as far as God is concerned, we are a holy people. We're a people made right with God, not just *a* holy people, but verse 3, *his* holy people set apart for him. Something I also say often to the people who work for the Message is, 'The most important thing you bring to the Message is not your great commitment, your great giftedness, or your great resource. The most important thing you bring to the Message is your holiness.'

The fourth thing that Paul encourages them with is that they were a cross-cultural people. He says there were people from everywhere in this church in Corinth. There's nothing like the body of Christ. The church in Corinth was a beautiful mix of wealthy merchants and former temple prostitutes and everything in between, all kinds of broken humanity, all together in this hurly-burly mix. There's nothing like the church of Jesus – only he can truly bring people together from every culture, every class, every society. And it works because of him. We're a cross-cultural people.

Fifth, we are a people who call on the name of the Lord. We don't just 'pray' if we're followers of Jesus. We call on the name of Jesus, our Lord. The most powerful force in the universe is available to us – the powerful name of Jesus. I wish we could see prayer the way the Lord sees prayer. It's not just 'have my little prayer time at the start of the day and ask God to bless this, bless that.' We call on the name of the Lord, the name of Jesus, by which hell shakes, by which anything is possible! We bring his name and his power into impossible situations. That's what we've been called to as God's sanctified, holy people set apart for him.

The sixth thing that Paul says in verse 3 – 'you've been enriched in every way with grace and peace.' You know there's a virus far more deadly than any pandemic – one which kills your soul. It's the pursuit of materialism, and all across the world people have contracted a disease called affluenza. They really believe just a little bit more will satisfy. But the only thing that will satisfy the human heart is more grace and more peace. Without grace and peace, a rich man is poor; with grace and peace, a poor man is rich. We are rich in Christ – 'in him we've been enriched in every way.' We have Jesus and guess what? The Bible says all God's promises are yes in Christ and you've got Christ. If you're a Christian, you're rich.

The seventh thing Paul says about the Corinthians is, they're a gifted people. 'You do not lack any spiritual gift', he says. How fascinating is that? Wow, what a church it must have been, with gifts of the Spirit flying off all over the place. Miraculous signs and wonders. Yet you can be gifted in every way and still carnal. That's why we've seen some of our most gifted leaders fall recently. We think that because they're so gifted they must be indestructible. Be very careful if you're super gifted – there's every chance you're prone to weakness in other areas of your life. And often, being that gifted guy or girl means you've got a target on your back for the enemy.

And then the eighth thing from these verses is they were an expectant people. It says in verse seven they were 'eagerly waiting for Jesus to be revealed.' I believe the Lord is not just looking for faith on earth, he's actually looking for expectant faith – being on tiptoes of faith that at any moment, the kingdom could break in and we could see Jesus move. In my home church, above the cross at the front of the church, it says 'Expect a miracle.' I love that – every time you come into this place or when you go out of this place, expect a miracle! Wouldn't it transform your day today if you expected you were going to see a miracle somewhere or other?

The ninth thing is, we're a reliant people. We rely on him to 'keep us firm to the end'. If we don't, we won't. If I don't rely on Jesus but try to do things in my own strength, I'm definitely going to blow it. But if I rely on Jesus, he can keep me all the way to heaven. It terrifies me that I could be that guy who, despite preaching to others, gets into heaven by the skin of my teeth, blows it between now and seeing Jesus face to face. I want to receive Jesus' 'well done'. I don't want to be the guy who messes it up and lets the side down with all sorts of carnage. I want to be someone who relies wholeheartedly on Jesus to take me all the way.

The final thing that Paul says as he lets them know who they are in Christ is, 'Come on guys, live up to who you are!' Stop all this nonsense that's holding you back. We're a people in fellowship with Jesus. What a word – 'fellowship'. It speaks to me of intimacy, of closeness, of shared interests. I'm in fellowship with the Lord Jesus Christ. He's my friend and he's my Lord. One name pops up in all nine verses we've just looked at. Guess what the name is? The Lord Jesus Christ.

It all starts with him and ends with him. Every blessing is from him. All we are starts and ends with Jesus. He's the source of every blessing. He's the reason we want to live up to who we are, because he's gripped our heart. The greatest prize in life is fellowship with him. That's what we're made for. Which is why this precious, called, sanctified, holy, cross-cultural, enriched, gifted, expectant, reliant people is meant to live differently. They're meant to stand out, they are meant to change the world. That's who you are. Come on, let's live up to who we're meant to be.

....

A PRAYER

Thank you, Lord, for letting us know who we are, and who we are in you. None of this is possible without you, but thank you that you've made it possible to be these people. We want to be those people who, by the Spirit, live this out vision in this day and age. So stir us up, and keep speaking to us through your Word.

Amen.

....

1 CORINTHIANS 1:10-17

UNDIVIDED: THE RECIPE FOR REVIVAL

1 CORINTHIANS 1:10-17

I appeal to you, brothers and sisters, in the name of our Lord Jesus Christ, that all of you agree with one another in what you say and that there be no divisions among you, but that you be perfectly united in mind and thought. My brothers and sisters, some from Chloe's household have informed me that there are quarrels among you. What I mean is this: one of you says, 'I follow Paul'; another, 'I follow Apollos'; another, 'I follow Cephas'; still another, 'I follow Christ.'

Is Christ divided? Was Paul crucified for you? Were you baptised in the name of Paul? I thank God that I did not baptise any of you except Crispus and Gaius, so no one can say that you were baptised in my name. (Yes, I also baptised the household of Stephanas; beyond that, I don't remember if I baptised anyone else.) For Christ did not send me to baptise, but to preach the gospel – not with wisdom and eloquence, lest the cross of Christ be emptied of its power.

If you track the history of the English Premier League, you find that it's almost always been won by one of four teams: Liverpool, Manchester United (of course!), Chelsea or Manchester City. These are the big, title-winning clubs of English football.

But something remarkable happened in 2016. A much smaller team, Leicester City, had just about scraped through from being relegated the season before. Coming into the season, statistically they were 50,000 to 1 to win the League. No one could have expected them to win it. But that's exactly what happened. Surprising all the experts, they beat the odds and went on to win the title. They definitely didn't have the best players. They didn't have the biggest budget. They didn't have a stadium on a par with the top teams. Yet

22

they won. And they did it on the back of an incredible spirit of unity of purpose.

The same thing happened a few decades ago in the European Championship, the biggest club trophy in the world. It's usually won by the 'same old, same old' teams – Real Madrid, Bayern Munich, Liverpool, Inter Milan, Manchester United (of course!). But then, suddenly, not for one season but for two seasons running, 1979 and 1980, a little team called Nottingham Forest won it.

There was something about great leadership there for sure, but there was also something about unity of purpose. The players were in it together. They gave everything for each other. There was an incredible season of belief and confidence, which meant they were able to achieve in a massive way.

If that can happen in the world of sports, imagine what could happen with a church that would come together in unity of purpose. This is what Paul is getting at here.

Over the next few chapters, Paul is going to be teaching the Corinthians and rebuking them about morality, spiritual gifts, money and more. But at the heart of the Corinthians' problems was deadly division. It still is for the church, 2000 years later. Nothing hinders the cause of Christ like a divided church.

Paul begins by invoking the name of Jesus: 'I appeal to you, brothers and sisters, in the name of our Lord Jesus Christ.' You don't get any stronger than that. He goes in hard, because he's so serious. It's not just a bit uncomfortable when we don't get on, it's hindering this gospel. It's rejecting who we are: we are one in Christ. Christian believers have a bond stronger than blood – we're brothers and sisters, we are one family and we're called to maintain the unity Christ has won for us.

Jesus' prayer for the church when he prayed for us in John 17 was this: 'I pray… for those who will believe in me through their message, that all of them may be one, Father, just as you are in me and I am in you. May they also be in us so that the world may believe that you have sent me' (verses 20-21). Just like his Lord Jesus, Paul knew there was something massively evangelistic about unity.

What do our divisions say to a world in need? How crazy that there are 40,000 Christian denominations in the world today – a world that's desperate to hear about the way, the truth, the life, a world that desperately needs to hear the one true gospel.

Paul could be writing this letter to so many squabbling congregations today. Millions of Christians have fallen out with the church. Not with Jesus, but with his church. Maybe you're reading this, and you know that's true of you, too. Maybe you feel like you're done with church, all that squabbling, all that nonsense, all that division?

But you'll never become the man or woman of God you're meant to be unless you connect with his church. Don't be that guy or girl who's chipped up with church. Don't get disconnected. Ask for supernatural grace and forgiveness and God will give it to you. Be the one who quietly, through it all, through all the flesh in the church, all the silliness, all the religion, brings Christians together.

Do you speak well of your brothers and sisters? Well, you should. Speak well wherever possible as it blesses the heart of God. When I see my kids, even now they're grown adults, getting on well together, it blesses me as a dad. When we get on, it blesses the heart of God.

Satan is called 'the accuser of the brethren', and that makes him the divider of the brethren. He will do anything to carve us up, so often at the heart of Christian division you'll find personalities. Do you recognise it where Paul writes, "'I follow Paul'; another, 'I follow Apollos'; another, 'I follow Cephas'; still another, 'I follow Christ.'?"

Ever heard people waxing on about the great leaders of the past, looking back to the glory days, the good old days… 'Oh, I remember when we had our senior pastor, our founding pastor. How great were those days? How glorious were those days!' Don't be like that!

How easy is it to focus on the dynamic personality, a guy like Apollos? Here's how he's described in Acts 18: 'a Jew named Apollos, a native of his Alexandria, came to Ephesus. He was a learned man with a thorough knowledge of the scriptures, and had been instructed in the way of the Lord. And he spoke with great fervour'. You can imagine getting in your car to go hear Apollos at New Wine, couldn't you? Apollos was the superstar preacher – much more dynamic than Paul, whose sermons sometimes sent people to sleep (Acts 20:9). It's easy to build a personality cult around a guy like Apollos.

And then there's Cephas – Peter. Maybe he represented Jewish Christianity. The kosher issue is still a hot topic at this point in the early church – check out Paul's writing in Galatians 2. Peter struggled to pull away from the Jewish religion and live in the new era of grace, and so slipped back into legalism. Some of the weirdest rules come out of the people who are supposed to be free, Holy Spirit-led people.

I'm old enough to remember the house church movement – what a move of God that was as God poured out his Spirit and churches were planted all over the nation. So many great things came out of that but some of it turned very weird as people added new rules and regulations and burdens. Paul warns against that, too.

Paul even warns against the personality cult of himself. He could easily present himself as 'the man of power for the hour.' 'I'm the guy who had the download from heaven on the road to Damascus. I'm the apostle. I'm the scripture writer...!' But no, Paul says, 'Don't follow Apollos. Don't follow Peter, don't follow me. Follow Christ!'

Paul always brings it back to the cross: 'For Christ did not send me to baptise, but to preach the gospel – not with wisdom and eloquence, lest the cross of Christ be emptied of its power' (v17).

The cross is what unites us. The cross is what defines us as believers. Paul says, 'Did I die for you? No! There's only one who died for us. His name is Jesus.' That's what made unity possible. He died for all believers, and there's the key to unity right there. It's all about Jesus. The more we look at him, the more we love him and each other.

When we really follow Jesus, we come to realise our schisms and cliques dishonour him, hinder his work and actually carve his body apart. Sometimes we think we're so clever, but if we saw it through Jesus' eyes, we'd run a mile from disunity.

It's like honey when Christians really come together in unity and it's all focused on Jesus. We realise that we must love each other, serve each other, forgive each other and speak well of each other because there's a bond stronger than blood: we're going to spend all eternity together.

Remember this: when you committed your life to Jesus, you didn't just commit yourself to a vertical relationship with him, you committed yourself to a horizontal relationship with me, and I committed myself to a relationship with you. Because when we committed ourselves to Christ, we committed ourselves to his body on earth.

Ask yourself today: have you become a bit chipped up about church? Maybe just a little bit disconnected in this season? Repent of that. Recommit yourself to your horizontal relationship with the body of Christ. If he's going to do anything on his earth, he's going to do it through me and you working together for his glory. Commit yourself to that relationship afresh.

Are there brothers and sisters who you've fallen out with? Those relationships really matter. Repent, reach out, do what you can. Allow the Holy Spirit to renew your thinking to transform your mind to see others with the love of Jesus, Jesus who would have died for that person if he or she was the only person he ever made. Love them with his passion.

Are there any who you've fallen out with or hurt you deeply in the body of Christ? Ask God to give you his grace. And he will, because he longs for his body to be united in mission and vision and purpose and passion.

A PRAYER

Lord, I pray you'll bring us together like never before.
Forgive us for the times we have been agents of disunity,
times we've said things about our brothers and sisters
that were out of order. Forgive us, Lord. We repent.

We long for your church to come together like
never before because we long for your name
to be made known. Unite us, Lord, around your
purposes for your glory. Thank you, Jesus.

Amen.

1 CORINTHIANS 1:18–31

THE UPSIDE-DOWN, BACK-TO-FRONT, RIGHT-WAY-ROUND GOSPEL

For the message of the cross is foolishness to those who are perishing, but to us who are being saved it is the power of God. For it is written:
'I will destroy the wisdom of the wise;
the intelligence of the intelligent I will frustrate.'
Where is the wise person? Where is the teacher of the law? Where is the philosopher of this age? Has not God made foolish the wisdom of the world? For since in the wisdom of God the world through its wisdom did not know him, God was pleased through the foolishness of what was preached to save those who believe. Jews demand signs and Greeks look for wisdom, but we preach Christ crucified: a stumbling-block to Jews and foolishness to Gentiles, but to those whom God has called, both Jews and Greeks, Christ the power of God and the wisdom of God. For the foolishness of God is wiser than human wisdom, and the weakness of God is stronger than human strength.

Brothers and sisters, think of what you were when you were called. Not many of you were wise by human standards; not many were influential; not many were of noble birth. But God chose the foolish things of the world to shame the wise; God chose the weak things of the world to shame the strong. God chose the lowly things of this world and the despised things – and the things that are not – to nullify the things that are, so that no one may boast before him. It is because of him that you are in Christ Jesus, who has become for us wisdom from God – that is, our righteousness, holiness and redemption. Therefore, as it is written: 'Let the one who boasts boast in the Lord.'

On this earth there are three types of people. There are those who try to get to God by seeking after signs. There are those who look to get there through wisdom – in other words, they try and do it in a human way. And finally, there are those who discover God through revelation. He does the work: God steps in and opens their eyes. It's actually the only way to salvation.

I'm seeing this beautiful thing happen more than ever at the moment. I'll wander over to our Community Grocery just next door and I'll chat with people whose eyes had just been opened to the gospel. It's so fresh, so exciting and so beautiful to them. And it's a marvellous thing to see, ordinary Wythenshawe folk who are getting hold of something that seems like foolishness to professors, even theologians.

Paul describes his life's work in four words in verse 22 – 'We preach Christ crucified.' And in a world of entertainment, how stupid preaching must seem.

I wonder if you saw Joe Biden's inauguration, back at the beginning of 2021. Even though the crowds were much smaller than usual because of Covid, what a show they put on. They had Katy Perry and Jennifer Lopez and Lady Gaga all doing their thing. But the person who stole the show was a young black woman called Amanda Gorman. She got up without fanfare, and shared simple but stirring words of poetry. She was amazing – she just owned the stage as she spoke words of peace, many from scripture. She made such an impact she went to #1 and #2 on the Amazon bestseller list overnight. We were reminded of the power of the spoken word. And how much more powerful can it be when ordinary men and women preach the message of the cross, the most powerful message in the world.

Our heart at The Message is to raise up globally an army of thousands of evangelists who say 'I preach Christ crucified. That's the call on my life.' With our Advance network, we are seeing thousands of evangelists being raised up in 80 nations, multiplying this precious gift.

Most of the apostles were defined by being unschooled and totally ordinary. They were rural, common people, but they went on to turn the world upside down. Paul, who wrote these words in 1 Corinthians, was quite different. In fact, he was the exact opposite. He was a Pharisee of Pharisees. He'd studied theology at the equivalent of the best university, under the greatest minds. So when Paul became a Christian, he had to unlearn so much so-called wisdom so that he could make known his crucified Lord.

That's why he describes the message of the gospel, this upside-down message, as 'a stumbling-block to Jews and foolishness to Gentiles, but to those whom God has called, both Jews and Greeks, Christ the power of God and the wisdom of God' (23-24).

The best defence of the gospel, I think, is its power. The great thing about the gospel is it works. It's the most powerful thing in the world – nothing else can change the human heart. You can criticise the message, you can criticise the church, but you can't take away what's happening in real people's lives.

We see it here all the time at The Message. Former drug addicts and alcoholics turned into role models and mentors because Jesus met them. People trapped in self-harm and abuse, broken and shattered, but set free because Jesus stepped in. Bad guys, gangsters, bringing chaos to everyone around them, destroying their own lives and their families, finding transformation because of Jesus.

It's the power of the gospel that does that – it's something that only God can do. We celebrate testimonies, stories like these, because only God can do these things. Jesus gets a lot of glory when we see him do the things that only he can do – when we see the power of God displayed, it is hard to deny the power of this gospel and Paul rejoices in it.

That's why some of our most powerful evangelists are people who have experienced dramatic transformation themselves. I think of Nick Shahlavi who had multiple suicide attempts as a teenager, was a drug dealer, living a chaotic, criminal life, and then Jesus stepped in. Now he's an amazing evangelist, working with us and seeing incredibly things happen through his ministry. Recently every single prisoner in Britain was delivered a CD by his band Vital Signs – his music went into every prison cell in Britain. They all had a chance to hear his amazing story, and we're believing more salvation will come through that.

Or I think about Lauren Jubb. It wasn't long ago that Lauren was standing in one of our Message gigs in Sheffield, with pills in her pocket, planning to take her own life. She was so lost, so broken until she heard the message of the cross and the power of God broke in. Now an amazing evangelist, Lauren runs sessions training young people in creative arts and as well as training them in rap and singing and dancing, she gets the chance to train them in the message of the cross and the glory of the gospel.

Part of the reason Christianity was so offensive to snobby, hierarchical Greco-Roman society was because of the way it spread amongst the poor and lower classes. It really was, and always has been, good news to the poor. Look at the heroes of the Bible – David the shepherd boy; Gideon from the smallest tribe; Mary, God's humble servant. They're not VIPs.

A few years ago at one of our big festivals, we put on what we called a 'VIP reception.' We got a big marquee and we invited with all the posh people we could think of – our rich donors, big name leaders from the church and civic society, people we reckoned had influence. The 'very important people.' The problem was, my brother Michael was back at that time from missionary service in Sudan. He was living in a mud hut, amongst the poor, serving them and following Jesus. Michael said to me, 'I'm not really sure about this VIP thing, Andy.'

I was brought up short, because we'd made the fatal mistake of thinking of the rich, the well-educated, the successful and the famous people as the VIPs. But who were Jesus' VIPs? Who was he most interested in being around, and spending his time with? There were tax collectors and sinners and broken people. The secret to Jesus' success was basically that he had friends in low places. Have we? In many ways, I believe it's the secret to The Message's success and will continue to be when God does the things that only he can do because,

'"… my thoughts are not your thoughts, neither are your ways my ways," declares the Lord. "As the heavens are higher than the earth, so are my ways higher than your ways and my thoughts than your thoughts' (Isaiah 55:8-9).

We must humble ourselves in order to do his work his way. Our way is always based on human effort, wise words, good deeds, trying to earn our credit in heaven. But his way is always 'Seek me. Call on me, return to me.' When we do that, we get these incredible gospel results and rewards. Honestly, nothing is impossible for those with a truly humble heart who do his work his way. The value of our work depends on God's gifts, not on our qualifications and credentials.

I'm glad of that today. If it was based upon my qualifications and credentials, I'd be stuffed. But that's not the way God works. He uses ordinary people to do extraordinary things for him and through him. When God gets hold of us, he can turn the world upside down through us, one life at a time.

....

A PRAYER

Thank you, Jesus, for the amazing gospel. It's so
different, so radical, so crazy, but so exciting. Raise
up many who others would look upon as foolish,
simple, ordinary people. Gift them and impassion
them and change the world through them, Lord. Do
it through us – because that's exactly who we are!

Thank you for this gospel that's utterly transformational
and which works in any situation. It's the power
of God for the salvation of anyone who believes.
We pray for a season of much salvation as you
reveal your wisdom, as you show your power.

Amen.

....

1 CORINTHIANS 2:1–16

TIME TO GROW UP

1 CORINTHIANS 2:1-16

And so it was with me, brothers and sisters. When I came to you, I did not come with eloquence or human wisdom as I proclaimed to you the testimony about God. For I resolved to know nothing while I was with you except Jesus Christ and him crucified. I came to you in weakness with great fear and trembling. My message and my preaching were not with wise and persuasive words, but with a demonstration of the Spirit's power, so that your faith might not rest on human wisdom, but on God's power.

We do, however, speak a message of wisdom among the mature, but not the wisdom of this age or of the rulers of this age, who are coming to nothing. No, we declare God's wisdom, a mystery that has been hidden and that God destined for our glory before time began. None of the rulers of this age understood it, for if they had, they would not have crucified the Lord of glory. However, as it is written:

'What no eye has seen, what no ear has heard, and what no human mind has conceived' – the things God has prepared for those who love him – these are the things God has revealed to us by his Spirit.

The Spirit searches all things, even the deep things of God. For who knows a person's thoughts except their own spirit within them? In the same way no one knows the thoughts of God except the Spirit of God. What we have received is not the spirit of the world, but the Spirit who is from God, so that we may understand what God has freely given us. This is what we speak, not in words taught us by human wisdom but in words taught by the Spirit, explaining spiritual realities with Spirit-taught words. The person without the Spirit does not accept the things that come from the Spirit of God but considers them foolishness, and cannot understand them because they are discerned only through the

Spirit. The person with the Spirit makes judgements about all things,
but such a person is not subject to merely human judgements, for,
  "Who has known the mind of the Lord
    so as to instruct him?"
  But we have the mind of Christ.'

....

Chapter 2 starts with Paul recalling his arrival in Corinth. He describes his response as he walked into this great, debauched city as one of 'fear and trembling.' What must Paul have thought as he looked at this sin-soaked city, dominated by a vast pagan temple served by a thousand prostitutes with all sorts of dodgy goings-on? On top of this, I expect the devil was whispering words of doubt into his head, too: 'You know you're no Apollos... You're not a man of power for the hour... people fall asleep when you preach, Paul!'

These two things can so easily weigh down a visionary leader – being overwhelmed by the size of the task and being doubtful of our own abilities. So Paul tells us he did what every leader needs to do at that moment – he made a conscious decision to abandon any natural gifts or worldly wisdom: 'I resolved to know nothing while I was with you except Jesus Christ and him crucified' (v2).

He knew where the road of worldly wisdom was going to take him. He'd been down that road already and basically he'd ended up trying to wipe out the church. So Paul chooses against worldly wisdom, and instead goes all-in for preaching the cross and demonstrating its power.

Imagine if we had more leaders like that! More Christian leaders who say, 'I'm just going to preach the simple message of the cross and believe that God's going to demonstrate his power through that message, that seems like foolishness to many but is life to those who are being saved' (cf. 1:18).

It reminds me of the first time I went to hear Billy Graham. I was a young evangelist in my early twenties, and Billy announced he was coming to Anfield as part of a tour of football stadiums in the UK. I booked several coaches in faith and invited everybody and anybody I knew to come along to hear Billy. I remember the coaches pulling up outside Anfield and joining the masses in the stadium. There were maybe 50,000 people there.

Personally I was so excited to be there – Billy was perhaps the greatest evangelist the world's ever known, at least in terms of numbers. He preached to more people face to face than anyone else in history as far as I know. The evening went off as planned – as always, there was some worship from Cliff Barrows and prayers from some bishops. Then Billy got to his feet. I was so excited to finally see the great man in the flesh.

And you know what? It was a little boring. It was so simple. His jokes weren't funny. It was a message I was sure I'd heard before. I was so disappointed. But then he said this, and I'll never forget it: 'And now I'm going to invite you to come down onto the pitch. Make Jesus Lord, turn away from your sins and you'll receive eternal life. And as I pray now, thousands of you are going to come forward.' I was, to say the least, a bit sceptical. 'After that sermon, Billy? I doubt it!', I thought.

And yet, as he prayed, I started to hear the seats flipping up. Thousands of people, including my mother-in-law who was sitting next to me, got up and walked down onto the pitch to give their life to Christ. It was just an amazing moment of the demonstration of God's power, the power of the cross. Billy had preached it faithfully, simply. He wasn't preaching for me, he was preaching for them. He was preaching to people for whom this was good news.

Paul knew, like Billy, that in this place called Corinth, this unchurched place, he had to keep it simple, he had to keep it cross-centred. He had to rely on the power of the gospel which can change any human heart. He was determined not to rely on his own wisdom. He decided to rely on the power of the cross.

Is Paul saying that all learning is wrong? Is it wrong to study theology, for example? No, definitely not. He's just determined at this point, when preaching the gospel in a place like Corinth (and like many of the places we minister in the UK and around the world) to keep it simple. In verse 6, he makes it clear that there is great wisdom to discover in God, but only once you've understood the foundational nature of the cross. So often we charge into theology without understanding that everything we need to know, we can know through the cross.

What makes us mature believers then? I think it's when we decide to be people who are self-controlled and patient, honest and compassionate, accountable, humble and others-centred. I know I'm not that man sometimes, but I want to be, because it's the mature leader that's going to go the distance and make a mark for Jesus. Paul recognises that the true mark of a mature believer is that they're defined by an eternal perspective. The more humble they become, the more heavenly their thoughts are. It's like the deeper we go, the higher we go, and the more amazing the good news becomes.

Paul understood that the life, death, resurrection, ascension and return of the Lord is not just for his glory but amazingly, it's for our glory, too. Look at verse 9 again: 'What no eye has seen, what no ear has heard, and what no human mind has conceived' – the things God has prepared for those who love him – these are the things God has revealed to us by his Spirit.'

Paul had a vision of eternity that made him want to live the mature Christian life, that made him want to keep the cross front and centre, that made him want to rely on the Spirit's power here and now. He's had a glimpse of how much God has saved for him.

Imagine the Lord at the beginning of time, creating the universe... We see his handiwork here on the Earth – beautiful vistas, things that take our breath away in creation. Well, the Bible says God has saved some things even better than that for us. At the dawn of time, he saved things we'll only see in heaven. Wow!

The greatest piece of classical music, as voted for by the public, is Barber's Adagio for Strings. What a beautiful piece of music. Well, the Lord's got way better than that for us when we get to see him face to face. The greatest pop song of all time, as voted by the public, is Hey Jude. Well, God's got way better than that saved for us too. God's even got thoughts saved for us that are better than any of the thoughts our minds have conceived here on Earth. When our minds and our imaginations get to think in a completely free, glorified way, it'll – literally – blow our minds!

Paul finishes this passage by reminding us that this is all ultimately a work of the Spirit. It's not primarily a work of mature, humble, accountable believers, it's a work of the Spirit. He says these things of God have been revealed to us by his Spirit. The Holy Spirit is being poured out all over the world in unprecedented measure so that ordinary people can understand the message of the cross. We just simply preach the cross in humility and the Holy Spirit kicks in and people receive eternal life. People start to live the right kind of life. People start to multiply it out. Real Christian faith is generated by the Spirit of God and lived in dependence upon the Spirit of God.

Spirit break out! Break out on a people who understand the cross are determined to share it in the power of the Spirit, a people who live for eternity and invite others into eternity. Populate heaven, plunder hell, God – be glorified all over the world at a time like this!

....

A PRAYER

God, will you generate faith in us, faith for salvation all over the world through mature disciples going out in the power of your Spirit. Help us, Lord, to live as if we're going to live forever – because of course we are.

Thank you, Jesus, that the future is bright. We may have trials this side of heaven, but heaven's going to be awesome and amazing. Thank you for the taste of heaven, the little down payment here on Earth we get in the Holy Spirit.

Amen.

....

1 CORINTHIANS 3:1-23

GROW UP... AND BUILD UP

Brothers and sisters, I could not address you as people who live by the Spirit but as people who are still worldly – mere infants in Christ. I gave you milk, not solid food, for you were not yet ready for it. Indeed, you are still not ready. You are still worldly. For since there is jealousy and quarrelling among you, are you not worldly? Are you not acting like mere humans? For when one says, 'I follow Paul,' and another, 'I follow Apollos,' are you not mere human beings?

    What, after all, is Apollos? And what is Paul? Only servants, through whom you came to believe – as the Lord has assigned to each his task. I planted the seed, Apollos watered it, but God has been making it grow. So neither the one who plants nor the one who waters is anything, but only God, who makes things grow. The one who plants and the one who waters have one purpose, and they will each be rewarded according to their own labour. For we are fellow workers in God's service; you are God's field, God's building.

    By the grace God has given me, I laid a foundation as a wise builder, and someone else is building on it. But each one should build with care. For no one can lay any foundation other than the one already laid, which is Jesus Christ. If anyone builds on this foundation using gold, silver, costly stones, wood, hay or straw, their work will be shown for what it is, because the Day will bring it to light. It will be revealed with fire, and the fire will test the quality of each person's work. If what has been built survives, the builder will receive a reward. If it is burned up, the builder will suffer loss but yet will be saved – even though only as one escaping through the flames.

    Don't you know that you yourselves are God's temple and that God's Spirit dwells in your midst? If anyone destroys God's temple, God will destroy that person; for God's temple is sacred, and you together are that temple.

Do not deceive yourselves. If any of you think you are wise by the standards of this age, you should become "fools" so that you may become wise. For the wisdom of this world is foolishness in God's sight. As it is written: "He catches the wise in their craftiness"; and again, "The Lord knows that the thoughts of the wise are futile." So then, no more boasting about human leaders! All things are yours, whether Paul or Apollos or Cephas or the world or life or death or the present or the future – all are yours, and you are of Christ, and Christ is of God.

....

All the best preachers use picture language in their talks. Not all pictures hold up over time, but I think Paul's do. I think they were highly relevant to the Corinthian church who heard them first, and they're still relevant for us today.

The first picture Paul uses to describe the Corinthian church is the picture of babies (verses 1-2). In the first few verses, he describes them 'infants in Christ', picturing them in spiritual nappies, still needing milk when by now they should have moved on to solid food.

Now, mother's milk is a marvellous, miraculous thing. When a baby is born, its mother produces this incredible milk called colostrum, a super-nutritious milk which gives a baby all sorts of a boost, helps its immune system and protects it against all sorts of diseases. It's just what the baby needs. Statistically babies who have their mother's milk are healthier later in life and that's a wonderful thing.

But there comes a time when it's right for every kid to move on from mother's milk. My mum and dad used to have these friends who you might politely call 'alternative'. They had a little boy who used to go out playing football and run around with his mates outside but would then run back inside the house, lift his mother's jumper up and 'latch on.' I never knew where to look! It was so embarrassing. Although feeding at his mum's breast was absolutely the right thing for this lad to do a few years before, now it was just wrong!

Could the same be true of some of our Christian behaviour? It's perfectly normal and right to act like a little baby when we first come to Christ, when we need feeding and building up and encouraging. For a while we need to just be looked after, like babies. But there comes a time when we have to grow up and move on to solid food. It's time some of us stop expecting to be spoon-fed in church on a Sunday morning and learn to feed ourselves. We need to move on to the more meaty stuff in the Word.

Paul calls out some of the hallmarks of the Corinthians' immaturity – jealousy and quarrelling, putting spotlights on individuals and playing one person off against another. Envy and jealousy in the church are like dirty nappies – they stink! Paul challenges them to grow up with this striking picture.

Babyish behaviour often comes through in our attitudes towards church, I think. 'I didn't get much out of church today' is a frighteningly immature thing to say. It's so selfish. Jumping from one church to another to try and 'get fed' is immature behaviour, too. Growing up means digging in, serving, and pouring our lives into others, not waiting to be spoon-fed by someone else. I don't want to be a baby – do you?

The second picture Paul uses to challenge the church is of planting and watering (verses 6-9). He wants them to see how ridiculous it is to think that anyone but God can produce growth. As if we human beings could bring about salvation! Only God can do that. So there's no point picking teams, being 'Paul people' or 'Apollos people' or 'Cephas people'. None of us human leaders are anything; only God brings the growth.

It's time to quit boasting about leaders, or whose team is the best, and focus on our miracle-working God. Yes, we all have a role to play. We turn over the field. We fertilise the field by faithful prayer, pressing in in the secret place. We plant the seeds of the gospel by faithful proclamation and faithful presence, loving people, coming alongside people in their need. But only God can make things grow. Only God can do the ultimate miracle of giving life, eternal life springing up as we do the right things.

And then Paul uses a third analogy – of foundations and buildings (verses 9-15). There are two ways to build, according to Paul – he describes them as building with precious things with gold and silver and costly stones, in other words, valuable materials that don't burn up. Or there is another way of building, with wood and hay and stubble – materials which cost much less but which will burn up quickly. It's clear to me he's talking about building a life or a ministry with costly things like humility, like generosity, like mercy. Like the ultimate symbol of the great cost at the centre of the Christian faith, the cross of Jesus.

I'm staggered sometimes that there are Christian ministries who will sign contracts for money from government or from other organisations on the basis that they don't share their faith. They'll do the good works but they'll sign away their birthright. That is never going to happen at The Message on my watch. We are never going to sign for a single penny if we can't share the good news of Jesus. It may look good now to go the other way – take the money and improve our numbers – but on the final day it won't last. It'll just be burnt up.

There is a reward according to the Bible when we get to heaven. There will be a judgement for Christians – not according to our sins, because Jesus has already been judged for our sins. But there will be a judgement for Christians, according to our good works, in other words what we've done with what's been entrusted to us. We won't lose our salvation but we may lose our reward.

The main reward we'll get, I believe, if we make eternal things a priority, is people. We'll see in heaven all those we've played a part in them getting there. We'll stand before Jesus and our chins will hit the floor when we discover how all our prayer, sacrificial giving and kindness was weaved together by God. And there'll be a welcome committee of people saying, 'You've played a part in me being here! What you built with your life has lasted! Thank you!' What a welcome some Christians will receive on that final day – what a prize!

But for some Christians, the Bible teaches, there'll be a bit of a deafening silence. It will become obvious that they've built in the wrong way – they built with wood and hay and stubble and it all just got burned up. You may have built a great business. You may have had a prosperous and successful life in worldly terms. But actually in eternal terms, you'll have failed.

I wonder if you remember, during one of our lockdowns, standing in the street cheering Captain Tom, the ninety-nine-year-old fundraising legend, after he died? Millions of people clapped him the day after he died. And, you know, well done, Captain Tom! It was a lovely moment. But I don't want the claps and the cheers and the whistles down here. I want them up there. I want to be welcomed in by people saying, 'Well done! You kept going when others gave up. You kept the cross central when there was pressure from secular society to water it down. You tried your best to lift high the name of Jesus, you loved the poor. You prayed, you gave yourself to the purposes of God.' And as a result, you receive the greatest reward – hearing Jesus, say, 'Well done, good and faithful servant. Enter into the joy of your master.'

Do you know what Jesus' joy is? Jesus' joy is heaven populated with people. 'For the joy set before him, he went to the cross.' He went to the cross imagining the millions of souls that would be saved through his great sacrifice. It was the only thing that made it worthwhile for Jesus. He was thinking about you and your family and your friends who could be in heaven because he paid the price to get them there.

So let's grow up. Let's leave behind babyish jealousy and competition and all that rubbish. Let's plant lots of gospel seeds. Let's fertilise the soil well – let's do everything we can to create an environment where, if God sees fit, he can allow millions of seeds to grow into eternal life.

Let's pray well, let's give people the gift of our presence and love people who are hurting. Let's boldly proclaim the gospel. Let's build well. Let's not just build pension pots and property portfolios and reputations and ministries – let's build for eternity.

....

A PRAYER

Lord, we want to grow up, to leave behind the babyish
behaviour that we can so easily slip into. We want to
be good sowers of this beautiful gospel seed. And we
want to build well, for eternity, on the firm foundation
of the cross and the resurrection and the ascension
and the return of Jesus, the firm foundation of this
gospel that works. Help us to be that kind of people.

Amen.

....

1 CORINTHIANS 4:1-13

LEADERSHIP
JESUS-STYLE

1 CORINTHIANS 4:1-13

This, then, is how you ought to regard us: as servants of Christ and as those entrusted with the mysteries God has revealed. Now it is required that those who have been given a trust must prove faithful. I care very little if I am judged by you or by any human court; indeed, I do not even judge myself. My conscience is clear, but that does not make me innocent. It is the Lord who judges me. Therefore judge nothing before the appointed time; wait until the Lord comes. He will bring to light what is hidden in darkness and will expose the motives of the heart. At that time each will receive their praise from God.

Now, brothers and sisters, I have applied these things to myself and Apollos for your benefit, so that you may learn from us the meaning of the saying, 'Do not go beyond what is written.' Then you will not be puffed up in being a follower of one of us over against the other. For who makes you different from anyone else? What do you have that you did not receive? And if you did receive it, why do you boast as though you did not?

Already you have all you want! Already you have become rich! You have begun to reign – and that without us! How I wish that you really had begun to reign so that we also might reign with you! For it seems to me that God has put us apostles on display at the end of the procession, like those condemned to die in the arena. We have been made a spectacle to the whole universe, to angels as well as to human beings. We are fools for Christ, but you are so wise in Christ! We are weak, but you are strong! You are honoured, we are dishonoured! To this very hour we go hungry and thirsty, we are in rags, we are brutally treated, we are homeless. We work hard with our own hands. When we are cursed, we bless; when we are persecuted, we endure it; when we are slandered, we answer kindly. We have become the scum of the earth, the garbage of the world – right up to this moment.

We're living in days, sadly, when it's all too common to hear stories of leaders who have 'fallen'. Men – and usually it does seem to be men – who have inspired us in the past, are all too often having 'moral failures' which not only bring down their lives but their ministries, too. It's heartbreaking, but history keeps repeating itself. You'd have thought we'd have learned by now that giftedness doesn't equal godliness, and that charisma doesn't always equal character. It's a lot easier to say the right stuff than to live the right life.

The truth is, according to Paul, and according to 1 Corinthians, wherever the church of Jesus Christ follows big names, it follows the world. Every breakdown, every moral failure, all the carnage, is all to do with us becoming man-centred rather than Christ-centred.

Responding to a recent situation of a public fall of a famous ministry leader, my friend and Message trustee Rob White, wrote this:

'The more we put people on pedestals, the less we're helping them to grow in their relationship with God. We shouldn't be surprised that those we idolise disappoint us. The very word 'idol' gives us a clue. If we change church culture so that we discourage people seeking the spotlight and we avoid creating heroes and heroines, we'll be less disappointed and we'll do our leaders a favour, too. The only people we've got a hope of knowing the character of are those we spend time with daily – those in our own church communities and neighbourhoods. We can look to them for inspiration and encouragement if we need to. Even then, history tells us that we could be disheartened if we pin our hopes on anyone, apart from

Jesus himself. It's good to see Jesus in and be inspired by the ordinary Christian, the gentle and the quiet. Those who love and serve God in their neighbour without telling anyone about it. In our current age, meekness goes against the grain, but true humility and Christlikeness will not disillusion us.'

That's powerful. We need to wake up to the upside-down nature of the gospel. We need to recover what it means to be disciples of Jesus. And I believe the desperate need of the hour is believers who are defined by two words.

The first word is 'servant.' Paul said, 'This is then how you need to regard us, as servants of Christ' (v1). In other words, 'Don't regard me as a "Senior Apostle" or "Right Reverend" or "Founder" or whatever. No, just use "servant".' In fact, the word Paul uses is stronger than servant – it's 'slave.'

In John 13 we get the perfect model for Jesus-style leadership. You probably know the story. At the Last Supper, Jesus just longed to spend some time with his mates, eating and sharing friendship with them so he'd booked the upper room. Of course in Jesus' day, they wore open-toed sandals. There were running sewers in the streets and there were donkeys doing their business, and you would arrive for your evening meal and you would lie prostrate. Your smelly feet would never be far from someone else's face.

And so there was always a slave. When you booked a room, the slave came as part of the package. It was the job for the most junior slave to wash people's feet on arrival so the guests could just sit back and enjoy the meal. And yet on this occasion, despite the room having been booked, there was no slave. And so the proud apostles, Jesus' men of power for the hour, all shuffled around, seeing what was going to happen. Nobody offered to wash the feet... until Jesus stepped up.

And it says this remarkable thing: 'Jesus knew that the Father had put all things under his power, and that he had come from God and was returning to God' (John 13:3). All things were under Jesus' power. He was the most powerful person in the universe. He knew it. He knew where he come from. He knew where he was going. That's how centred Jesus was at this point in his life. He knew what was going happen in just a few hours' time. But he was totally focused on the Father. He was totally secure in his identity with God.

Here's how it continues: 'So he got from the meal, took off his outer clothing, wrapped a towel around his waist, and after he poured into a basin, he began to wash the disciples' feet' (verses 4-5). Jesus was so secure, he could take on the role of a servant. We know the disciples' reaction – horror! But after doing this amazing thing, Jesus goes on to say this: 'You call me 'Teacher' and 'Lord,' and rightly so, for that is what I am. Now that I, your Lord and Teacher, have washed your feet, you also should wash one another's feet. I have set you an example that you should do as I have done for you' (13-15).

Michael Baughen was the Bishop of Chester for many years. In public, he would often wear these extravagant bishop outfits – the tall hats and the long robes and the shepherd's crook made of gold. It obviously had an effect on people and how they treated him – and even how he thought about himself. He told me once that in order to help him remember who he was, so he didn't get puffed up, he used to keep a small piece of towel in his pocket. Any time he put his hand in his pocket, he would feel this piece of towel and remember that his job as a leader in the church was first of all to wash other people's feet – in other words, to serve them.

Like Jesus, Paul and Apollos knew who they were. They were aware how others saw them – 'the scum of the earth, garbage in the world.' They were homeless, travelling missionaries who'd given it all up for Jesus, sacrificed everything. But this made them rich, in total contrast to the puffed-up Corinthians. They knew they were rich, so they could happily serve. They could happily obey Christ and take on the role of servants because they knew what they'd been saved from. They knew they'd been forgiven, and that their pasts were dealt with. They knew where they were going. They knew they'd started already to 'reign and rule' with Christ. What can touch a person like that? What's the point of somebody like that being puffed up and trying to push and shove for profile? They could truly be servants.

The second word you could use to describe leadership Jesus-style in 1 Corinthians 4 is 'stewards'.

We are people, who've been 'entrusted' (v1), given a trust. This phrase would be very common in Paul's day – it is the phrase used to describe an overseer or a housekeeper of somebody else's stuff. Again, this was often a slave. The job of the steward is to care for somebody else's stuff. Your master is rich – you're not. You've just been given his stuff to care for and to look after.

Well, that's what a Christian is, of course. We don't own anything, we're just looking after it for someone else – God! We can get a little bit obsessed with how much stuff we have in this world. While I was writing this, we were in a season where house prices were shooting up in the midst of the pandemic. And I heard a lot of Christians talking about how much their house was worth. I felt like saying, 'It's not your house, it's his house! He owns everything. You're just a steward looking after the house on his behalf.'

Sometimes I wonder if our teaching on tithing in the church gives the impression that once we've given our 10% or whatever, we're free to do what we want with the rest. No! It's all God's – 100% of it is God's! Anything you've got is a gift from him, and, like Paul, we should be aware that at some point we'll have to give an account for our stewardship of his stuff.

And it's not just about money. It's also about how well we steward what God has given us in his Word. In Hebrews 13:17 the writer says, 'Have confidence in your leaders and submit to their authority because they keep watch over you as those who will have to give account.' And James 3:1 says this: 'Not many of you should become teachers, my fellow believers because you know that we who teach will be judged more strictly.' That gives me the shivers! If that's the standard, I'm not sure I want to teach anymore!

Paul says that for him, an apostle, it means not 'going beyond what is written' (v6). We will be judged on whether we go beyond anything that's written in God's Word. I daren't remove things from God's Word that I don't like because they don't fit in with my priorities or my lifestyle choices. I simply cannot do that. I am a steward of the Word of God. I daren't go beyond what's written. God given us a book. It's his faithful, fruitful, wonderful Word. It's the Word of God. The Bible is the most precious thing this life affords. I daren't take away from it. I don't want to add to it. I simply have to be a good steward of the Word of God. We all need to pray that our leaders are good stewards of the Word of God – that they teach the Bible faithfully because it's the Word of life.

....

A PRAYER

Holy Spirit, we ask you to illuminate our hearts and show us how we can be better servants, whatever that costs – serving others and serving you. And show us how we can be better stewards of all the gifts you've given us.

Especially, Lord, we want to be faithful stewards of the Word that you've given us. We pray that we can be faithful stewards for the glory of your name, because you deserve it.

Amen.

....

1 CORINTHIANS 4:14-21

MUMS AND DADS
IN THE FAITH

1 CORINTHIANS 4:14-21

I am writing this not to shame you but to warn you as my dear children. Even if you had ten thousand guardians in Christ, you do not have many fathers, for in Christ Jesus I became your father through the gospel. Therefore I urge you to imitate me. For this reason I have sent to you Timothy, my son whom I love, who is faithful in the Lord. He will remind you of my way of life in Christ Jesus, which agrees with what I teach everywhere in every church.

Some of you have become arrogant, as if I were not coming to you. But I will come to you very soon, if the Lord is willing, and then I will find out not only how these arrogant people are talking, but what power they have. For the kingdom of God is not a matter of talk but of power. What do you prefer? Shall I come to you with a rod of discipline, or shall I come in love and with a gentle spirit?

I wonder if you ever remember hearing your Mum say those fatal words, 'Wait till your father gets home!' There's a little bit of that going on here, I think. 'I'm sending Timothy now, but wait till your spiritual father gets home!'

It gets me thinking about spiritual mums and dads, how important they can be to us, and how game-changing it would be if the church could fully embrace the power of having, and being, mothers and fathers in the Lord.

One of my spiritual dads when I was a brand-new Christian in my late teens was a man called Val Grieve. He looked a bit like Eric Morecambe and to me was just as funny. He was a senior partner in a law firm here in Manchester and in his spare time he was involved in just about every good thing that the Lord was doing in the city.

He was major player in the unity movement and had a hand in the Catacombs Trust, a radical youth movement in the city centre. He also was the chairman of Operation Mobilisation, involved with buying George Verwer's first couple of ships.

Val was such an influence on my life. It was amazing to me that this super-busy, super-influential guy took me under his wing as a brand new, scruffy Christian. Not only did I go to a Bible study with him and a few other lads, he set up a prayer school to teach us how to pray on a Sunday afternoon. He'd have us round for dinner at his house, which had the best library of Christian books you've ever seen. He had a serious reputation as a preacher and whenever he went out to preach, he would always take some of his 'spiritual sons' with him to lead the service or give our testimonies. He just poured his life into us. I was so blessed to have had Val Grieve as a spiritual dad as a baby Christian.

In terms of spiritual mothers, I'm blessed to be able to name my own Mum. What an influence she's had on my life! She's never wavered – rock-solid prayer, passion and encouragement through all sorts of challenges in her life. She lost her own dad in very tragic circumstances, and then my Dad went to heaven when my Mum was in her mid-50s, but she stayed fiery and passionate for God through all of it. She prays for me and The Message more than any other person. I'm so blessed to have a spiritual Mum like that.

So who were yours? Who are your spiritual mothers and fathers? Everyone should have them, I believe. People who invest in you. It's the way church is meant to work.

The way the name 'father' is used in some Christian settings is weird and can even be wrong. It can be very exclusive, all about the priest and his status. It can mean one man doing all the work of ministry, disabling lay ministry and the ministry of women. It can water down evangelism and church unity. But I'm not talking about that kind of 'father' – I'm talking about fathers and mothers in the faith who are a massive blessing.

Paul goes on to say something in the next verse that's either like the height of presumption or hugely challenging for any of us who have any kind of role of fatherhood or motherhood, any sense that other people are looking to us for some help and instruction, he says, 'Therefore, I urge you to imitate me' (v16). What a thing to say!

The truth is, the key way to measure the health of any church or ministry is what kind of sons and daughters are being raised up. Are you raising up people who are like you? And if you are, is that a good thing? Remember the church isn't about buildings or budgets primarily. It's about ordinary people showing one another how to follow Jesus. Remember the church in Corinth didn't have a New Testament. Part of the New Testament was about to land on their doorstep – the first letter to the Corinthians – but everything else they had to see in someone else. They had to see faith in Jesus embodied, even more than we do. They had to see in the flesh what it looks like to be a Christ follower.

How we model faith to one another is crucial. Mature mothers and fathers raise mature sons and daughters, who become mothers and fathers to others. Are we raising up sons and daughters like that? If we are, we're going to change the world.

We talk a lot here at The Message about our 'Message family.' I like the fact that some people think of The Message as a family. Of course we don't want it to get weird and exclusive but there is something about a call to journey together with people who become like family to you. There's a bond there that's stronger than blood. We're united together in this thing called the church. So we should resolve things in a different way than we have to with other people because we're family – we're mothers and fathers, sons and daughters.

A report recently from the US showed that senior pastors of churches are having a shorter and shorter tenure in the job – the average used to be seven years but, over the last decade, it's gone down to four years. I'm sure that's the same in the UK as well. Barna, who produced the report, said it's inspired by an upwardly-mobile, number-crazed mentality which increasingly seems to plague pastors of churches. Isn't that the spirit of the age? People are always looking for the next thing, the better move, the better ministry. But it shouldn't be that way in the family of God. The church is in a mess in lots of places – and no wonder if leaders are chasing after that! Chasing after numbers and profile and prestige, looking upon ministry as a career choice, is toxic.

We desperately need the church to be a place where we can be fathered and mothered by people who love us deeply in the Lord and who model faith for us like Paul did for Timothy. We need leaders who realise that talk is cheap. Paul says, 'The kingdom of God is not a matter of talk, but of power' (v20). They may boast about having 'ten thousand guardians' (v15) – the kinds of leaders who can talk a good talk and perhaps they can let you hear what your itching ears want to hear. But the Lord is looking for leaders who look to the power of the Spirit, the power of the gospel to save, the power of gospel to change the world. Those are the kind of leaders, the kind of mothers and fathers, we need. Basically, mothers and fathers who raise up kids like Timothy. What a thing for Paul to say about Timothy: 'He's my son, whom I love. He's faithful in the Lord' (17).

When I get to heaven, I'm so looking forward to meeting Val Grieve and my Mum there. And I long for them to say, 'Well done, Andy. You've been faithful in the Lord. You've had a go. Well done mate.' Won't that be amazing? I want my spiritual mothers and fathers to welcome me in. But even more than that. I want to see many sons and daughters who I've had the opportunity of investing in and I can welcome them in. I'll be able to say, 'Well done! You've kept going to the end and look what Jesus has got for us!' What a day that will be.

Who are your mothers and fathers in the faith? If you haven't got people who regularly invest in you, who mentor you, who train you, who believe in you, who see you at your worst then patch you up and send you out again... if you haven't got that kind of mum or dad in the faith, get one!

What about if you've been a Christian for a bit longer? Why don't you reach out to some young man or woman who needs fathering or mothering in the faith – and tell them you'd love to bring out the very best in them? There are many young people who've had terrible mums and dads in the past and that's holding them back from being the best they can be in Christ. You could change all that by showing them what a true godly role model, a fun-filled mum or dad in the faith, looks like.

....

A PRAYER

Thank you Lord, for the people who have invested
in us – the people you brought along our paths to

make us who we are. I pray that those of us who are a bit older, a bit further on in the faith, will be role models of godliness and passion. We want to be men and women who love your Word and live it out.

And for those of us who are younger in the faith and who need people to be mothers and fathers to us, and help us and love us with a deep love of Jesus, I pray you show us who those people are.

Amen.

....

1 CORINTHIANS 5

HOW TO POLARISE AND PARALYSE THE CHURCH

It is actually reported that there is sexual immorality among you, and of a kind that even pagans do not tolerate: a man is sleeping with his father's wife. And you are proud! Shouldn't you rather have gone into mourning and have put out of your fellowship the man who has been doing this? For my part, even though I am not physically present, I am with you in spirit. As one who is present with you in this way, I have already passed judgement in the name of our Lord Jesus on the one who has been doing this. So when you are assembled and I am with you in spirit, and the power of our Lord Jesus is present, hand this man over to Satan for the destruction of the flesh, so that his spirit may be saved on the day of the Lord.

Your boasting is not good. Don't you know that a little yeast leavens the whole batch of dough? Get rid of the old yeast, so that you may be a new unleavened batch – as you really are. For Christ, our Passover lamb, has been sacrificed. Therefore let us keep the Festival, not with the old bread leavened with malice and wickedness, but with the unleavened bread of sincerity and truth.

I wrote to you in my letter not to associate with sexually immoral people – not at all meaning the people of this world who are immoral, or the greedy and swindlers, or idolaters. In that case you would have to leave this world. But now I am writing to you that you must not associate with anyone who claims to be a brother or sister but is sexually immoral or greedy, an idolater or slanderer, a drunkard or swindler. Do not even eat with such people.

What business is it of mine to judge those outside the church? Are you not to judge those inside? God will judge those outside. 'Expel the wicked person from among you.'

Imagine this in the early days of the global pandemic: you are desperately ill with COVID-19. You're so badly ill, you need to go to hospital. You turn up the hospital feeling like death and you're sure they're going to take you straight into intensive care. But instead, the doctor welcomes you with a big hug. He doesn't have a mask on – in fact there's no PPE at all. Then he takes you straight into the ward full of elderly people and starts introducing you to them.

There'd be something there wrong, wouldn't there? The doctor might be acting carefree, but you know what he's doing is really scary. You know the virus is going to spread that way. He might call it freedom, but you know it's really dangerous.

That's a bit like what Paul is getting at here in Chapter 5. He doesn't use the analogy of a virus, but he uses something very similar to talk about sexual sin. He says it's like yeast. If you put a little bit of yeast into dough, you can't see it because it's so tiny. But it quickly spreads throughout the entire loaf and affects absolutely everything.

Paul knows that a virus is entering the church in first-century Corinth – and a virus is entering many churches in 21st-century Britain and around the world. It will polarise people and, if not dealt with, will paralyse the mission of the church. And it really matters.

Paul has heard about immorality of the worst kind in Corinth: a man sleeping with his own mother, and the church has done nothing about it. This is strictly forbidden in Leviticus 18. How can this kind of stuff go on in the church? Surely this can't be the church of Jesus?

But it's not too far from our world, is it? Recently one of the leading Christian apologists in the world was discovered to be a multiple offender in the most horrendous way. Catholic priests have been convicted for abusing little boys, and Anglican bishops for the most gross kind of paedophilia.

And it's even closer to home than that for many of us – as close as our own mobile phone. The word Paul uses for immorality is 'porneia', from which of course we get our word 'pornography'. Satan has a successful tactic that he's proven works again and again – strong temptation in sexual matters. And with the invention of the mobile, he's running riot. He's destroying more lives than ever through porneia.

You don't believe me? Talk to my mate whose dad was the chief executive of a Christian charity and yet who had a secret life of illegal pornography. Eventually he took his computer in to have it fixed and the shop reported him to the police. He was arrested and the shock of it destroyed his life. As a result, my friend set up Naked Truth, a Christian charity to help the millions of Christians who are addicted and struggling with pornography (thenakedtruthproject.com).

Back in Corinth, we learn they weren't just putting up with this stuff – some of them were proud of it, and I wonder how that could be. Surely no one could be proud of incest – proud of flagrantly immoral sexual activity? But maybe they were proud of being the ultimate 'Extreme Grace' Church. Maybe they were proud of being non-judgemental. In the midst of a sex-obsessed society, maybe it was easier not to call out sin as sin.

Maybe they were proud to have this guy as a member of their church? Maybe the man who was committing this sexual sin was a wealthy donor to the church? Maybe he was a kind of celebrity? Sometimes we treat people like that differently – one rule for big donors and celebrities and one rule for everybody else. That's wrong, Paul says. He tells them to root it out before it spreads through the church, confusing, dividing and paralysing the church.

So this is how the apostle deals with it: 'So when you are assembled and I am with you in spirit, and the power of our Lord

Jesus is present, hand this man over to Satan for the destruction of the flesh, so that his spirit may be saved on the day of the Lord' (4-5).

What's that all about? We're not surely about kicking people out who are sinners, are we Paul? Well, at the extreme level, says Paul, yes we are. He's not at all talking about outsiders. We're to be incredibly welcoming to outsiders. They're the very people we're trying to reach for Jesus. They're the very people who need the hope that comes in the gospel. But there is a clear expectation that once you've bowed the knee and made Jesus your Lord and chosen to live a life under the authority of his Word, you'll strive to live like it. We're not forcing anyone to become Christians. But when we do invite people to follow Jesus and make him Lord, we need to call them to repentance, as he does. Because repentance is the doorway to blessing.

My friend Mike Pilavachi did an epic interview with J John which I think everyone should watch. Mike put it like this. He said, when he became a Christian, wherever it was 40 years ago he was given the Bible as our authority for life and living and joy and freedom. So we did the things it says in the Bible. And we didn't do the things that it says in the Bible not to do. We allowed the Bible to judge us. But now, he says, we have a culture growing, especially among young adults where instead of bowing the knee to the Bible, they're judging the Bible. Instead of allowing the Bible to judge them, they're judging the Bible.

This is nuts. The Bible gives us the life of freedom and joy and breakthrough, and it is so different it's opposite to so much of the values of the world. And that's what we're buying into. That's what we're inviting people into as evangelists, and we must make the call to repent, make Jesus Lord. For the kingdom of heaven is at hand. And if there are extreme cases in the body of Christ amongst believers who call themselves Christians who will not repent when we challenge them over their sin, we actually have to kick them out of the church. That's what Paul says. For their own good and for the good of the church, it needs to be rooted out.

Any parent who refuses to discipline his kids is not being kind to them, but actually unkind. Any friend who has an addicted friend who doesn't do everything he can to help them through the addiction is not a friend to them. We have tragically lost some who have come to Christ in prison who, when they've got out, have gone back to the drugs and the chaos and ultimately they've lost their lives. I'm thinking of one guy in particular. We did everything we could to challenge him about his lifestyle and help him, but he chose to go the destructive way. I fully expect to see him in heaven, but what a mess. What a waste of all the fruitfulness and all the blessing that could come through his life!

Whatever you do, do not move away from the Bible's teaching and the authority of the church. Do not move away from accountable relationships. If you do, you're an accident waiting to happen. Being in the church, part of the body, sent out on mission is the safe place for a Christian to be. It is scary out there and Satan just wants to gobble you up, mercilessly. When we're isolated, we're vulnerable. It's like being dropped off defenceless in enemy territory. It's time to wake up. Make Jesus Lord afresh, come back and be restored.

....

A PRAYER

Lord, we don't want to get taken out by the enemy
through sexual sin. We want to run the race marked out
for us all the way to glory. I pray for anybody reading

this who's getting sucked into sexual temptation, especially around pornography. Help them to repent, find good accountability, get good things in place.

Help us to live by a different standard – we've been called to a high calling to follow you. Jesus, let us be those people who live right and go after you. Thank you, Jesus.

Amen.

1 CORINTHIANS 6

TRUE FREEDOM

If any of you has a dispute with another, do you dare to take it before the ungodly for judgment instead of before the Lord's people? Or do you not know that the Lord's people will judge the world? And if you are to judge the world, are you not competent to judge trivial cases? Do you not know that we will judge angels? How much more the things of this life! Therefore, if you have disputes about such matters, do you ask for a ruling from those whose way of life is scorned in the church? I say this to shame you. Is it possible that there is nobody among you wise enough to judge a dispute between believers? But instead, one brother takes another to court – and this in front of unbelievers!

The very fact that you have lawsuits among you means you have been completely defeated already. Why not rather be wronged? Why not rather be cheated? Instead, you yourselves cheat and do wrong, and you do this to your brothers and sisters. Or do you not know that wrongdoers will not inherit the kingdom of God? Do not be deceived: Neither the sexually immoral nor idolaters nor adulterers nor men who have sex with men nor thieves nor the greedy nor drunkards nor slanderers nor swindlers will inherit the kingdom of God. And that is what some of you were. But you were washed, you were sanctified, you were justified in the name of the Lord Jesus Christ and by the Spirit of our God.

"I have the right to do anything," you say – but not everything is beneficial. "I have the right to do anything" – but I will not be mastered by anything. You say, "Food for the stomach and the stomach for food, and God will destroy them both." The body, however, is not meant for sexual immorality but for the Lord, and the Lord for the body. By his power God raised the Lord from the dead, and he will raise us also. Do you not know that your bodies are members of Christ himself? Shall

I then take the members of Christ and unite them with a prostitute?
Never! Do you not know that he who unites himself with a prostitute is
one with her in body? For it is said, "The two will become one flesh."
But whoever is united with the Lord is one with him in spirit.

Flee from sexual immorality. All other sins a person commits are
outside the body, but whoever sins sexually, sins against their own
body. Do you not know that your bodies are temples of the Holy
Spirit, who is in you, whom you have received from God? You are not
your own; you were bought at a price. Therefore honour God with
your bodies.

Do you know what the most important thing you bring to your
church is? It's not your gifts or your amazing creativity, not even
your passion. It's your holiness – your desire to be like Jesus. But I
know I'm never going to be able to give you a desire to be holy. No
amount of preaching is going to give you a desire to be holy. Rules, if
you're not careful, just rub up the old nature. We need grace.

As Paul goes on speaking to the Corinthian church, calling out
more behaviour that's out of order for Christians – various sinful
practises that were taking place, lawsuits among believers, sexual
immorality and wrong views of marriage – I know I've got to
remember which covenant I live in. I live in the era of grace. I'm not
trying to earn my salvation through good works. I'm saved through
grace alone by faith alone in Christ alone.

One of the most powerful ways God pours out his grace on us is
when he gives us a vision of holiness that makes us want it more than
anything else. Recently three things happened to me to illuminate
why I want to be holy, and I found them so helpful to read alongside
1 Corinthians 6.

The first thing was that I went to see my Mum, and she showed me an old diary entry from the 1970s. She'd copied down a little devotional on Philippians 2:13, 'God is at work in you both to will and to work for his good pleasure.'

It was called 'Obedience, a new approach' and it said this: 'We don't usually connect obedience with pleasure. More, necessity or fear? At the point of salvation, however, God built into you a 'want to' factor. Obedience is elevated in the Christian to a joyful response to all God has done for you. You don't have to manufacture it, but you do have to cultivate it and activate it. Serve the Lord with gladness. Anything else is merely outward compliance. We have a hard layer of obeying the desires of the flesh which has to be removed by the Holy Spirit, then we're receptive to God's will. It's the love of Christ that then compels us. Our relationship with God motivates us, not cold rules, or an "ought to" reluctant approach.'

That's powerful. It's our pleasure, our delight to serve the Lord with holiness, and set ourselves apart for his purposes. I heard a Christian leader recently trying to justify some sexual practises that are expressly forbidden in the Bible and this Christian leader said 'I had to find myself. I had to discover who I was.' But that's not what Jesus said. He said, 'Whoever finds their life will lose it, but whoever loses his life for my sake will find it' (Matthew 10:39). Die to yourself, and die to your sinful nature, and you'll start to live what Jesus calls 'life to the full' (John 10:10).

The second thing was that I received a video from the chairman of the Luis Palau organisation in the UK. Luis died in March 2021 and he was an amazing evangelist right to the end of his life. During his final weeks in hospital, he ministered powerfully to many people, including the surgeon who cared for Luis in his final days in palliative care. It made me think about why I want to be holy.

The surgeon's name is Gary Hart and here's part of what he said: 'I want to tell you a little bit about how I got to meet Luis Palau and have been blessed by him. Luis, of course, is very warm and in a short time I felt very welcome, even having no previous relationship with him. We shared some prayer and scripture together and I was greatly encouraged. What I found was that I always had to wait in line in his room because I'd go into his room and he'd be talking to the dietician who was there to get his lunch order and he would be asking her about her life. Or I'd go in and the physical therapist didn't want to leave because after his session they had more to talk about and Luis would be sharing things with him.

'One morning as we were starting our rounds, the night nurse was crying by the nurses' station. Another nurse friend who's a believer up there asked her, "Why are you crying?" and she said, "Oh, I had a marvellous experience in room 838. This patient with a terminal disease asked me about the difficulties in my life, and as he encouraged me, he said, "Why don't you come be in heaven with me?" And she was moved to tears and was sharing that experience with us. And it reminded me how we have an opportunity to be flesh and blood for Christ in the places where we work.'

Wow – there was a man who was truly living for eternity! I love that simple question to that nurse: 'Why don't you come to heaven with me?' – that Luis wants those to be the last words coming out of his mouth. 'Come and join me, come and be made holy, be made righteous, be like Christ.'

Our time on earth is our only chance to choose holiness. In eternity we'll be made holy – we won't have a choice! But right now we have this enormous privilege of being obedient, setting ourselves apart for Christ, choosing holiness.

The third thing that happened to me was that I had the privilege of interviewing Nicky Gumbel for one of our prayer days. Here is another beautiful man of God with a twinkle in his eye and the love of Jesus in his heart.

During the interview Nicky said, 'I've done 92 Alpha courses now. I've never once invited the Holy Spirit to come and he hasn't come. You know, sometimes it's been super dramatic, and other times it's just been like a gentle breeze.' And he reminded me of those scriptures from Luke 11 where it says, 'If you then, though you are evil, know how to give good gifts to your children, how much more will your Father in heaven give the Holy Spirit to those who ask him!'

So of course, I asked him to pray for the Message team. Nicky asked us to put our hands out and he invited the Holy Spirit to come and fill us afresh. I nearly fell off my chair in the office! It was really amazing, but it made me think, we need the power of the Spirit to make us receptive to God's will. There's no chance of living right by willpower, by just gritting our teeth – we'll just rub up against the old nature. We need the power of the Holy Spirit within, the Holy Spirit who gives us deep desires to be like Jesus!

Paul has been gripped by a desire for holiness because of his vision of eternity. He wants the Corinthian church to see what he sees – that we'll be holy one day. And because of that, he wants them to live in the beauty of holiness and express true worship, and because we have the Holy Spirit in our heart, who wants day by day to make us more like Jesus.

....

A PRAYER

Lord, we pray for a fresh desire to live right – to live
for Jesus, to live in the true freedom that comes
from turning our back on sin and turning to Jesus.

Help us, Lord, to be men and women set apart
for you that can shine in this world. Thank you for
people who show us what it looks like to shine for
you all the way to the very doorway of heaven.

Holy Spirit, fill us afresh and give us
deep desires to live right for you.

Amen.

....

1 CORINTHIANS 7:1-16

LET'S TALK ABOUT SEX... AND FASTING

1 CORINTHIANS 7:1-16

Now for the matters you wrote about: "It is good for a man not to have sexual relations with a woman." But since sexual immorality is occurring, each man should have sexual relations with his own wife, and each woman with her own husband. The husband should fulfil his marital duty to his wife, and likewise the wife to her husband. The wife does not have authority over her own body but yields it to her husband. In the same way, the husband does not have authority over his own body but yields it to his wife. Do not deprive each other except perhaps by mutual consent and for a time, so that you may devote yourselves to prayer. Then come together again so that Satan will not tempt you because of your lack of self-control.

I say this as a concession, not as a command. I wish that all of you were as I am. But each of you has your own gift from God; one has this gift, another has that.

Now to the unmarried and the widows I say: It is good for them to stay unmarried, as I do. But if they cannot control themselves, they should marry, for it is better to marry than to burn with passion.

To the married I give this command (not I, but the Lord): A wife must not separate from her husband. But if she does, she must remain unmarried or else be reconciled to her husband. And a husband must not divorce his wife.

To the rest I say this (I, not the Lord): If any brother has a wife who is not a believer and she is willing to live with him, he must not divorce her. And if a woman has a husband who is not a believer and he is willing to live with her, she must not divorce him. For the unbelieving husband has been sanctified through his wife, and the unbelieving wife has been sanctified through her believing husband. Otherwise your children would be unclean, but as it is, they are holy.

But if the unbeliever leaves, let it be so. The brother or the sister is not bound in such circumstances; God has called us to live in peace. How do you know, wife, whether you will save your husband? Or, how do you know, husband, whether you will save your wife?

The Christian faith runs on twin tracks: belief and behaviour. Right belief results in right behaviour; wrong belief always results in wrong behaviour. Paul knew this well, so he addresses what right behaviour looks like for a Christian from the starting point of good doctrine.

In these next few chapters of 1 Corinthians, Paul is obviously responding to questions from the church. It's a bit frustrating really – it's like we only get to hear one side of a telephone call. The church has written a letter to Paul asking a whole bunch of questions. We can hear what Paul's saying, but we're not always quite sure what exactly the Corinthians are asking.

But clearly the question at the start of Chapter 7, comes from people who had been saved out of incredibly debauched lifestyles. Corinth was like Las Vegas and Magaluf in one, but worse. There were prostitutes everywhere, including – in fact especially – in the temple. Before they became Christians, some of the church at Corinth would have been involved in worship that was basically just a mass orgy with 1,000 temple prostitutes. No wonder they had a debauched, debased view of sex.

Perhaps some of them were saying to Paul that surely the best thing now for them would be to steer clear of sex altogether now, and to remain celibate. But Paul says no, because sex is God's idea. It's a beautiful gift to be enjoyed in God's way – in a committed marriage relationship between a man and a woman. Recently I read some research which turned the prevailing wisdom about sex on its head.

Guess which people are having the most fulfilling, enjoyable sex lives? They're married men and women who are in a monogamous committed relationship. What a shock – the Bible works!

As he answers these questions around sex, Paul makes three powerful statements about marriage. The first thing he says is that polygamy is wrong. In Corinth that statement would have been shocking because it seemed so narrow. I can imagine Paul being under fire for it in this culture – one man and one woman saving themselves for marriage, not allowed to sow their wild oats wherever they wanted? Yet we live in a culture that's moving away from that faster and faster. It seems impossible to watch a Hollywood movie or Netflix series today without seeing couples jump into bed at the first possible opportunity. Our public leaders are no longer held to a high standard. It wasn't long ago that if you were a senior politician and you were involved in immorality or adultery, your career was over. Sadly we all know that this is no longer the case.

I'm shocked by how quickly we're moving away from the Bible. We need to be people who say no, the Bible is the Word of God, and moving away from the Word of God is devastating and destructive for our society. I believe we're already reaping some of the whirlwind of that.

The second thing that Paul stresses is the sexual rights and expectations of a husband and a wife. He says in verse 4: 'The wife does not have authority over her own body, but yields it to her husband.' And I can imagine some people rolling their eyes and writing off Paul as either really outdated or worse, misogynistic. But guess what? The very next thing he says is, 'In the same way the husband does not have authority over his body, but yields it to his wife.'

This was utterly revolutionary two thousand years ago, completely countercultural. Women were treated in Corinth as little more than chattel on most occasions, to be used for a while and moved on from. But right here Paul sets up a higher standard, a different way. Basically, he says, there's absolute equality in Christian marriage, worked out by mutual submission. It was completely new, completely radical at the time but it's proved to be the best building block for successful societies in the history of the world.

A third thing Paul says in answer to this question is he actually encourages abstaining from sex at certain times, so that couples can 'devote themselves to prayer.'

I've literally never heard of anyone doing that – have you? I know it's not very likely you're going to go on Facebook and announce it to the world. But it is interesting, isn't it, the way we pick and choose scriptures. We focus on the bits we like and we completely ignore bits that that don't seem relevant to us.

I became a Christian in an amazing youth group where God was on the move and every week people were coming to Christ. I went to a church that had a very high view of the Bible and taught the Bible faithfully. But I don't think for the first ten years of my Christian life, I was ever taught anything about fasting. It just wasn't on the radar. And yet the Bible teaches all the way through about the necessity of fasting. It seems there are some things you only get in this life through fasting and devoted prayer. It must have seemed frankly ridiculous to some of the Corinthians in their culture, but fasting is so important and so good for us, and Paul goes on to bring some helpful teaching on fasting generally, not just sex.

First thing he says, if you're going to fast sex, both of you must be in agreement. The word the Bible uses is literally 'in symphony'. I love that picture of two people coming together 'in symphony', setting themselves apart, devoting time to the Lord, denying themselves of their strongest passions because they want to have more passion for Jesus.

Here at The Message we have seasons where we encourage the whole movement to devote themselves to prayer and fasting. And I love that picture of 'in symphony' like a beautiful orchestra, all fasting different things and all praying in different ways but making a beautiful sound to our God in heaven as we come together and show him how seriously we want him to move in this generation.

The next thing about fasting is, Paul says, it's specifically to devote yourself to prayer. There is no point in fasting if you're not going to pray. If you're married, commit yourself in a fresh way to pray and fast with your spouse for breakthrough in your family and in your situations. If you're not married, find a prayer partner. There's power in agreement, especially in fasting together.

The last thing that Paul says here is once the season of fasting is over, get back to it. Satan is a schemer. He wants to steal every good gift. He wants to make things that are so beautiful and so precious. He wants to rob us as a couple being called to be committed to one another as one flesh. There's a beautiful outlet for burning passion – sex in marriage. It's good, it's holy, and Satan wants to rob us of it.

Satan deliberately concentrates so much of his activity on sexual temptation because it's been so successful for him. I was on a call recently with a bunch of leaders across Manchester and a guy shared with us about a leader of a large church who had fallen and had to step down from ministry. The ministry was falling apart and there was, as always, huge heartbreak and devastation for his family. The guy leading the meeting said something like this: 'Guys, if you're involved in any of this kind of behaviour, please confess it. Please repent of it. Come alongside someone, come alongside me or somebody you trust. Turn away from it. Go the opposite direction because it will find you out and it will be devastating. I promise you.' You could hear a pin drop on the call. We all knew we never wanted to find ourselves in that position.

So maybe there's someone reading this and right now you're involved in adultery and immorality, sexual infidelity – and you're trying to hide it. You might be thinking you'll get away with it, but you won't. It will be found out and it will be devastating. So today, turn to a brother or sister you trust. Repent and confess it, hard as that might be. Start to rebuild something before your world and your life comes crashing down.

What a precious thing it would be if when I get to heaven I meet someone who says, 'That paragraph in that book saved my marriage and that saved my reputation and I was able to stay with my kids.'

The beautiful thing about Jesus is, he's not here to hit you with a big stick into living a life of purity. He wants you to embrace a life of full joy, full freedom, full excitement. That's the kingdom life that Jesus has got for you. Why would you want anything else?

....

A PRAYER

Jesus, it's so easy to be swept along in the currents
of this culture but we choose not to be. We only
want to be swept along by your ageless truths and

by the currents of your Holy Spirit. We choose to turn away from anything that displeases you.

I pray for any brothers and sisters who are involved in immorality or adultery, and whose lives are going to come crashing down unless they do something about it, unless they repent, seek forgiveness and restoration. Please give people courage to do just that. We choose freedom and we choose joy and we choose you, Jesus, because you're amazing.

Amen.

1 CORINTHIANS 7:17-24

YOUR HEAVENLY ASSIGNMENT

Nevertheless, each person should live as a believer in whatever situation the Lord has assigned to them, just as God has called them. This is the rule I lay down in all the churches. Was a man already circumcised when he was called? He should not become uncircumcised. Was a man uncircumcised when he was called? He should not be circumcised. Circumcision is nothing and uncircumcision is nothing. Keeping God's commands is what counts. Each person should remain in the situation they were in when God called them.

Were you a slave when you were called? Don't let it trouble you – although if you can gain your freedom, do so. For the one who was a slave when called to faith in the Lord is the Lord's freed person; similarly, the one who was free when called is Christ's slave. You were bought at a price; do not become slaves of human beings. Brothers and sisters, each person, as responsible to God, should remain in the situation they were in when God called them.

The day you gave your life to Christ, you received two amazing gifts from Jesus. The first was salvation – the most precious gift in the world. The second great gift was good works. The triune God – Father, Son, Holy Spirit – already had plans for you and that day you were at last able to enter them. You could suddenly be what you were made for, because suddenly you were right with God and the potential was there for you to pour out your life on his good works. I call it 'your heavenly assignment' – good works designed by God for you to do. And Paul talks about it in this next section of this amazing book.

The greatest religious barrier in the early church was circumcision and the greatest social barrier was slavery. So a major question the new Gentile Christians were asking Paul was: 'Do we need to be circumcised?' And you can imagine them holding their breath, can't you? Especially the lads.

And then there's this strange question. Should we be uncircumcised? Apparently there was some kind of early version of cosmetic surgery where guys could attempt to be uncircumcised to show how they were free from the shackles of Judaism. So when Paul says these words, you can imagine the early Corinthians punching the air... 'Circumcision is nothing and uncircumcision is nothing. Keeping God's commands is what counts. Each person should remain in the situation they were in when God called them' (verses 19-20).

This must have really wound up the religious posse. The Pharisees were alive and well in AD50 or so and they're alive and well today – people who love to put rules and heavy burdens on new believers. What a joy to receive this word from Paul: you're free in Christ, stay as you are! This is a new era. It's all about relationship, not religious rules and regulations. I'm glad about that.

So on to the second question: What if you're a slave, Paul? And here we're not talking about the hideous African-American slave trade. We're talking about bondservants – people who gave themselves over to a master and would be in his service for a season. What if you're a bondservant and you get saved? Does that mean you should be set free? Should Christian masters be setting all their slaves free?

Paul's answer might not have excited the Corinthians quite as much. He says, 'Each person should remain in the situation you're in when God called you. Were you a slave when you were called? Don't let it trouble you, although if you can gain your freedom, do so.' What Paul is saying basically is this: be content as you are. God knows where you are. He knows where he needs you right now. Don't struggle and strive. Just accept that God's placed you where you are.

Paul was able to say this remarkable thing in Philippians 4: 'I know what it is to be in need and know what it is to have plenty. I've learned the secret of being content in any and every situation, whether well fed or hungry, whether, living in plenty or in want. I can do all this through Christ who strengthens me' (verses 12-13).

There are the words of the richest man who's ever lived. Godliness and contentment is what it's all about. This is the secret! And it still is a secret to many Christians who are always struggling and striving for more. When you can learn to be content, you're the freest person who's ever lived. You can be free in a prison cell or free in a palace.

Thinking about all this, I came across a mighty prayer from John Wesley, the most significant Christian of the 18th century, the last great revival that shook the nation. The culture was turning away from God. Historians say the nation was on the verge of civil war and Britain was getting drunk on gin. And then John Wesley got on his horse. He rode around Britain for 500,000 miles and a massive revival came.

John Wesley was an Anglican minister who had served God faithfully, even going abroad on mission trips. But he was depressed, discouraged and defeated until one day in Aldersgate Street in London, he felt his heart 'strangely warmed' as he encountered the power of the Holy Spirit. On the back of that encounter with Jesus, he wrote this famous prayer, the Wesley Covenant Prayer:

"I am no longer my own, but thine.

Put me to what thou wilt, rank me with whom thou wilt.

Put me to doing, put me to suffering.

Let me be employed by thee or laid aside for thee,

exalted for thee or brought low for thee.

Let me be full, let me be empty.

Let me have all things, let me have nothing.

I freely and heartily yield all things

to thy pleasure and disposal.

And now, O glorious and blessed God,

Father, Son, and Holy Spirit,

thou art mine, and I am thine. So be it.

And the covenant which I have made on earth,

let it be ratified in heaven. Amen."

That's a revival prayer right there! That's the kind of prayer that changes the world! Regularly Methodist people would pray this prayer and fully surrender their lives to Jesus, whatever that looked like, and on the back of people praying and living that prayer, living with godliness, in contentment, whatever the situation, revival came. Churches weren't just full, society was transformed. Education, healthcare, politics – every sector of society. That's real revival. On the back of this revival, missionaries were sent out to every nation on earth, and the gospel exploded.

It's said that Wesley was the most influential Christian of the 18th century. Our hero here at The Message, William Booth, was probably the most influential Christian of the 19th century. He had exactly the same heart – going after the poor and the lost, embracing suffering for the gospel. I wonder who the most influential Christian of the 20th century was? Some people would say Billy Graham.

That's not a bad shout – a man who for decades preached the gospel to more people than any man who's ever lived. All sorts of ministries were birthed on the back of Billy Graham's laid-down life. But actually, I think it was another Bill who was the most influential Christian of the 20th century.

Bill Bright founded Campus Crusade for Christ in 1951. He'd started to do gospel ministry amongst students in California, where he lived with his wife Vonda. The night he launched it in 1951, they wrote in the front of their Bibles, 'From this day forward we are slaves to Jesus Christ.' They signed it and they wrote the date – they meant it.

Bill Bright wrote a little tract to help reach university students and called it 'Four Spiritual Laws.' It's maybe not the best tract ever written, but God seems to like it. Two and a half billion copies later, it's still being used by God. Then he thought he'd make a film about Jesus, thoroughly based on the book of Matthew, where every word is from the scriptures. It was released into cinemas and it lost loads of money. But it turned out God had his hand on Bill's life because he was determined to be a slave to Jesus Christ. That film has now been translated into 1,790 languages. The Jesus Film is by a mile the most watched film in history, seen by billions. This very day, in all sorts of remote places they'll be putting the generator on, swinging the video screen up, watching the Jesus Film in their own language and repentance will be happening. Probably thousands more people today will be won for Christ through that film.

What started off with just two of them in 1951 now has 19,000 missionaries. It's the world's largest mission agency, and it's in almost every country on the Earth. It all started with a prayer: 'From this day forward, I'm a slave to Jesus Christ.' I believe Bill Bright's incredible impact on the world, not just in his own time transforming society, but sending missionaries out to the far ends of the earth, was all birthed in a prayer: 'Whatever it takes from this day forward, I'm going to choose to be a slave to Jesus Christ. I'm not going to hold on tightly to things; I'm going to hold on tightly to this gospel. It's all about Jesus.'

As I close this chapter, maybe you'd like to pray John Wesley's prayer and make it your own?

....

A PRAYER

I say to you, Jesus, from this day forward, I am a slave to Jesus Christ. I'm no longer my own, but yours. Put me to what you will, rank me with whom you will. Put me to doing, put me to suffering. Let me be employed for you or laid aside for you, exalted for you or brought low for you. Let me be full. Let me be empty. Let me have all things. Let me have nothing. I freely and wholeheartedly yield all things to your pleasure and your disposal. And now glorious and blessed, God, Father, Son and Holy Spirit, you are mine and I am yours. So be it. And the covenant now made on earth, let it be ratified in heaven.

Amen.

....

1 CORINTHIANS 8:1-13

KNOWLEDGE PUFFS UP, LOVE BUILDS UP

Now about food sacrificed to idols: We know that "We all possess knowledge." But knowledge puffs up while love builds up. Those who think they know something do not yet know as they ought to know. But whoever loves God is known by God.

So then, about eating food sacrificed to idols: We know that "An idol is nothing at all in the world" and that "There is no God but one." For even if there are so-called gods, whether in heaven or on earth (as indeed there are many "gods" and many "lords"), yet for us there is but one God, the Father, from whom all things came and for whom we live; and there is but one Lord, Jesus Christ, through whom all things came and through whom we live.

But not everyone possesses this knowledge. Some people are still so accustomed to idols that when they eat sacrificial food they think of it as having been sacrificed to a god, and since their conscience is weak, it is defiled. But food does not bring us near to God; we are no worse if we do not eat, and no better if we do.

Be careful, however, that the exercise of your rights does not become a stumbling block to the weak. For if someone with a weak conscience sees you, with all your knowledge, eating in an idol's temple, won't that person be emboldened to eat what is sacrificed to idols? So this weak brother or sister, for whom Christ died, is destroyed by your knowledge. When you sin against them in this way and wound their weak conscience, you sin against Christ. Therefore, if what I eat causes my brother or sister to fall into sin, I will never eat meat again, so that I will not cause them to fall.

At first glance, 1 Corinthians 8 might not strike us as exactly essential reading. Christians arguing over food sacrificed to idols? That might have been relevant to people 2000 years ago but it's hardly a big issue in my church today! But as we dig in, I think we'll find it's super relevant to what's going on in the church today.

Two thousand years ago in Corinth there were two groups in the church – and both are alive and well in the church today. They are the 'rules' group and the 'licence' group. Today they might be arguing about what certificate of film it's OK for a Christian to watch, whether a Christian can drink alcohol or not, whether Christian kids should go out trick-or-treating, or whether they should read Harry Potter books. Back then, they were talking about food sacrificed to idols.

At the centre of Corinthian society was this vast temple to the goddess Diana, with 1,000 temple prostitutes and all sorts of sordid sexual activity as part of their worship. There was also a massive amount of meat being sacrificed, to try and get on the right side of the pagan gods. This meant that rather than going to the meat market to buy your meat, you could get cheap leftovers from the temple, because there was always masses of meat going to waste.

It was a divisive issue for believers back then. They knew what went on in the temple so some believers refused to eat it on the grounds that it wasn't pure – it had been offered to false gods and idols and it was therefore tainted in their eyes. Other Christians saw it differently: 'It's just meat. I'm free because Jesus has died for me.'

So Paul speaks right into this situation and says yes, of course you're free to eat meat. You've got that knowledge, but there's a higher call for Christians every time. It's the call of love. Love that trumps my rights every time. You know that you can do it, but you're not going to do it, if it's going to hurt your brother or your sister.

That's what Paul means when he says knowledge on its own puffs up, but love builds up.

Love needs to characterise everything about us as followers of Jesus. Think about the way you use social media. Do you not think it's quite shocking the way Christians can flaunt their knowledge on social media, tearing down other brothers and sisters in the process? Imagine if Christian social media could be full of love and building up and encouraging rather than this rubbish that so many people are putting out there. There's nothing wrong with knowledge. It's just that flaunting it is so horrible without love. Flaunting our knowledge can so easily make us proud, which is the root of all kinds of sin. Paul says basically it's not about how much theology you know, nor how much you know about God. It's about how much you're known by God that matters.

If you're truly in a relationship with Jesus, love is going to characterise everything about you. Your first thought is going to be love and support and encouragement, especially for new Christians, especially for weaker brothers and sisters. So Paul says, if you're truly living a humble Jesus-centred life, you'll be known by this.

'Be careful that the exercise of your rights does not become a stumbling block', he writes. We live in a society marked by our rights and everything that we deserve – especially where I live, in one of the wealthiest nations in all of history with so many toys and trinkets. We can so buy into the media marketing machine, can't we? McDonald's tells us that you deserve a break. L'Oreal tells us that you're worth it. I saw a holiday advert recently, saying, 'Get the holiday you deserve.' The times we live in make us think we deserve so much. But the Bible calls us to lay down our rights for the love of others.

You may have heard of Jim Elliot. He famously went out to reach the Waorani tribe in eastern Ecuador in 1956, and was murdered as soon as he arrived by the pagan tribes people. Soon after, his wife Elizabeth went to the same tribe that had martyred her husband, and gave herself to reaching them for Jesus. She said, 'I've given up my rights to a nice home, a nice husband...' and she listed all the things she'd given up, her rights. 'I've laid it all down for the sake of knowing Christ.' Imagine if there were more believers like her.

Yes, God may allow us to have a nice house or a nice husband or a nice wife. But it's not your right! You laid down all your rights when you came to Christ. There's nothing greater than knowing Jesus – knowing him and being known by him is what makes life worth living. We need to reflect on who our role model in all this is. Look how Paul describes Jesus in verse 6. He says, 'there is but one God, the Father, from whom all things came and for whom we live; and there is but one Lord, Jesus Christ, through whom all things came and through whom we live.'

Wow – some people say the Bible doesn't say Jesus is God, but right there, Paul says Jesus is God – he says he made all things, he's holding all things together by his powerful word. That's our Jesus! You're only alive because he said so. You only took your last breath because he allowed it. He will wind up world history by his powerful word. Our whole lives should be spent praising him and acknowledging how glorious he is.

And yet in Philippians this is what it says. Christ Jesus, 'who, being in very nature God, did not consider equality with God something to be used to his own advantage; rather, he made himself nothing by taking the very nature of a servant, being made in human likeness.

And being found in appearance as a man, he humbled himself by becoming obedient to death – even death on a cross!' (2:6-8)

That's our Jesus. From that place of awesome power and authority, he left heaven and came to earth. Not just being born in a stable, but dying the criminal's death that was brutal and hideous – taking the punishment that we deserve. Sometimes we need to reflect on that. And that alone. Our Jesus didn't jostle and push forward, but was willing to take the place of a servant.

We're not going to flaunt our knowledge when we look at Jesus. We're going to live the life of love and prefer others. We're going to really care about others' feelings, no matter how free we feel in certain situations. We're going to prefer others because Jesus, our ultimate role model, did exactly that, all the way to the cross.

....

A PRAYER

Help us Jesus to understand your call to take up our cross. We have decided to follow you, Jesus. We give up our rights for something far greater – that beautiful relationship of knowing you and being known by you. I pray that you will mobilise and motivate a people all over the world to make the most of this extraordinary season we're living in.

We want to please you and serve you and in the midst of it all, we want to be a church that's full of service and love and pushes others forward to living the life of love that builds others up too. So help us, Holy Spirit equip us, and fill us for that great task.

Amen.

1 CORINTHIANS 9:1-27

FAMOUS LAST WORDS

1 CORINTHIANS 9:1-27

*Am I not free? Am I not an apostle? Have I not seen Jesus our Lord?
Are you not the result of my work in the Lord? Even though I may not
be an apostle to others, surely I am to you! For you are the seal of my
apostleship in the Lord.*

*This is my defence to those who sit in judgement on me. Don't we
have the right to food and drink? Don't we have the right to take a
believing wife along with us, as do the other apostles and the Lord's
brothers and Cephas? Or is it only I and Barnabas who lack the right to
not work for a living?*

*Who serves as a soldier at his own expense? Who plants a vineyard
and does not eat its grapes? Who tends a flock and does not drink the
milk? Do I say this merely on human authority? Doesn't the Law say
the same thing? For it is written in the Law of Moses: "Do not muzzle
an ox while it is treading out the grain." Is it about oxen that God is
concerned? Surely he says this for us, doesn't he? Yes, this was written
for us, because whoever ploughs and threshes should be able to do so in
the hope of sharing in the harvest. If we have sown spiritual seed among
you, is it too much if we reap a material harvest from you? If others
have this right of support from you, shouldn't we have it all the more?*

*But we did not use this right. On the contrary, we put up with
anything rather than hinder the gospel of Christ.*

*Don't you know that those who serve in the temple get their food
from the temple, and that those who serve at the altar share in what is
offered on the altar? In the same way, the Lord has commanded that
those who preach the gospel should receive their living from the gospel.*

*But I have not used any of these rights. And I am not writing this
in the hope that you will do such things for me, for I would rather die
than allow anyone to deprive me of this boast. For when I preach the*

gospel, I cannot boast, since I am compelled to preach. Woe to me if I do not preach the gospel! If I preach voluntarily, I have a reward; if not voluntarily, I am simply discharging the trust committed to me. What then is my reward? Just this: that in preaching the gospel I may offer it free of charge, and so not make full use of my rights as a preacher of the gospel.

Though I am free and belong to no one, I have made myself a slave to everyone, to win as many as possible. To the Jews I became like a Jew, to win the Jews. To those under the law I became like one under the law (though I myself am not under the law), so as to win those under the law. To those not having the law I became like one not having the law (though I am not free from God's law but am under Christ's law), so as to win those not having the law. To the weak I became weak, to win the weak. I have become all things to all people so that by all possible means I might save some. I do all this for the sake of the gospel, that I may share in its blessings.

Do you not know that in a race all the runners run, but only one gets the prize? Run in such a way as to get the prize. Everyone who competes in the games goes into strict training. They do it to get a crown that will not last, but we do it to get a crown that will last forever. Therefore I do not run like someone running aimlessly; I do not fight like a boxer beating the air. No, I strike a blow to my body and make it my slave so that after I have preached to others, I myself will not be disqualified for the prize.

....

In the last days of his amazing life, one of my absolute heroes, Luis Palau, recorded a short video for his friends and team. In it, you can tell his body is fading, but his spirit is strong. With some of his last

119

breaths on earth, he draws out three words from 1 Corinthians 9, which he wanted to be ringing in our ears. Here's what he said:

'I'm not going to say anything that's really new. I want to use an old passage in 1 Corinthians 9. Three words: woe, win and run. "Woe to me if I don't preach the gospel," the apostle says (16). Pastors, you and I, woe to us! There's plenty to do. The virus has opened many doors. Number two, win. Five times Paul says "win". He wants to win people to Christ. He says, "I become all things to all men, so that by all means I may save some." He knows not all are going to be saved, but he sure tries. So woe, if I don't preach. Win as many as possible. And the third one: "Run and get the prize." RUN, get the prize. In other words, it's good to aim for the Lord's approval. And the Lord's plan is, "Well done, you good and faithful servant".'

How beautiful – and I honestly believe Luis received those precious words from Jesus and now he's experiencing all the eternal pleasures at Jesus' right hand that he saves for people like Luis, who give their all for him.

Luis was a man who was free. He was free to stay at home with his wife and kids, but he chose to travel the world preaching the gospel. He was free to pursue a career as a lawyer and have many more material possessions than he had, but he chose the way of the evangelist. He gave it all up for a prize. He knew that there was a prize that trumps everything else – those words, 'Well done, good and faithful servant'. Elizabeth Elliot knew it too – that's why after her husband was martyred she went back to the very same tribe. She said, 'I've laid down my rights.'

This was Paul's testimony, too. In 1 Corinthians 9 in the first few verses, Paul makes it clear he's an apostle. He's seen the Lord. He planted the church. He's got plenty of rights as the senior leader. He's got the right to earn a living from the church. He's got the right to respect. But he was willing to say this: 'I don't use this right' (v12) On the contrary, he was willing to put up with anything rather than hinder the gospel of Christ. What else is he supposed to do? 'For when I preach the gospel, I cannot boast, since I'm compelled to preach the gospel. Woe to me, if I do not preach the gospel' (v16).

God, give us more evangelists with that heart and that passion. Evangelists like Jeremiah, who with everything coming against him could say this: 'The word of the Lord has brought me insult and reproach all day long. But if I say I will not mention his word or speak anymore of his name, his words are like a fire, a fire shut up in my bones I'm weary of holding in, indeed I cannot' (Jeremiah 20:8-9).

You see, Paul didn't do this for a job – this was the very passion of his life. I remember in the very early days of The Message, when there were just a few staff we took on an amazing singer. She was a lovely woman of God, but I was devastated when she said to me one day, 'Andy, this is just a bit of a stepping-stone for me. It's just a job working for The Message.' How can you be like that? How can it be that you could be involved in something like The Message without believing it's your calling, your passion? If you can't say, 'Woe to me if I don't preach the gospel'?

Paul modelled single-minded discipleship in his desire to win people to Christ. As Luis said, the word 'win' comes five times in this passage. Paul excluded no legitimate means to win people for

Jesus. I want the same to be true of us. Our groceries, our bands, our buses, our teams... Prisons, Eden and Advance – they're all about winning people for Jesus. It's a platform to win people for Jesus – we're a movement that's focused on winning people for Jesus by all and any means.

I remember going out to Holland when we first started doing big gigs, way back in those early days with World Wide Message Tribe. We played at a Dutch festival and we met some people who were a little bit shocked that a Christian band could use dance music, the music of the night clubs. I enjoyed telling them, 'Can't you see that you can use any kind of music as a platform?'

But then as I wandered around this festival I found a little side stage, where there was this horrific band covered in tattoos, long greasy hair and leather jackets, playing death metal music. In my opinion, the worst kind of music! I thought, 'This is appalling. Call themselves Christians? How can they play that kind of music?' Until someone said to me, 'You really need to meet the guys.' So I went backstage and met this band and they were goths who'd been saved from that culture who were now planting churches in caves, using death metal in a beautiful way to win this community for Jesus. 'All things to all men to win some,' Paul says.

William Booth, who as I mentioned already is a massive hero of ours at The Message, said, 'Beginning as I did with a clean sheet of paper, wedded to no plan, willing to take a leaf out of anyone's book, above all to obey the direction of the Holy Spirit, we tried various methods and those that did not answer we unhesitatingly threw overboard and adopted something else.'

Our calling as Christians is to find the model that brings the greatest integrity alongside the greatest impact, and throw everything at it to win as many as possible for Jesus. That's what The Message is about. That's what every church and every ministry should be about. And Paul goes on to write this amazing, famous sentence: 'I've made myself a slave to everyone to win as many as possible' (v19).

Sounds like Jesus, doesn't it? It sounds like our Jesus who was willing to leave the place of glory and come as a servant, a slave to all to win as many as possible. Isn't he amazing? And he did it to win you, to win you back to heaven to win a place in eternity, to win the prize of a life that counts.

Here's what Martin Luther said: 'A Christian is the most free lord of all and subject to none. But a Christian man is also the most dutiful servant of all, and subject to all.'

Because Paul was compelled to preach the gospel and win as many at all costs, he was determined to 'run to win the prize' (v24).

Now, I've never run a marathon. The furthest I've run is 10K and that felt like a very long way. The nearest I've got to running a marathon is actually running a marathon feeding station. (I know, it's not too impressive!) When you run a marathon feeding station you see thousands of runners going past and most of them you're slightly worried that they might collapse and die halfway around. They come huffing and puffing past you and you're glad to give them their water and their energy bar and cheer them on. Their prize is just stumbling over the finishing line several hours later, to make the distance and be happy to tell all their friends about it.

There are some Christians whose prize is just to get through life, to keep going to church, to keep praying and reading the Bible and finally get into heaven. But there are other Christians who are a bit more like Mo Farah. The first guys who come past you at the marathon feeding station are lean, super-fit guys with incredible focus. You can't believe the speed they're running at consistently for over 26 miles. Mo Farah's training regime was insane – he ran 130 miles a week, nearly a marathon every day, plus lots of strengthening and conditioning. He punished himself because he was going after a prize. I guess he also knew that if he didn't do it, his rivals would. So he put his whole body on the line day after day, seven days a week to win that race, to win that prize. A prize that, of course, will perish!

What about us? How much are we willing to push ourselves to run the race to win the prize, to win the 'well done' that Luis talked about? Are we willing to push ourselves and run – sacrificial prayer and fasting, outrageous generosity, witnessing for Christ? Running the race marked out for us because we've got our eyes on the prize? We've got our eyes on the 'Well done'?

We know only what's done for Jesus will last, and our great prize is heaven populated and hell plundered. Our great prize is glory to Jesus here on the earth. This place, where there are sinners and there are the lost and the broken, and they're hurting, there'll be none of that in heaven.

This is our one chance in all eternity to run with perseverance, the race marked out for us (Heb 12:1). It's what made all Paul's sacrifices and sufferings seem like 'light and momentary troubles' because they were earning for him an eternal glory that far outweighed them all' (2 Cor 4:17).

I wonder what your last message to your friends and family will be, if you get to do such a thing, maybe to your team if you're involved in leadership, or just to your family. It's not a bad one to be able to say woe to me if I didn't preach the gospel, if I didn't focus on winning people for Jesus. To be able to say, I've run the race, I've fought the fight and now all that awaits me is the crown.

It really is the only life that counts. We know it in our hearts, don't we? If we know Jesus, we know there needs to be a greater urgency in us. I want to be a man who, with Luis Palau, with Paul, says, 'Woe to me if I don't preach the gospel.' I'm prepared to become a slave to all to win people for Jesus. I want to run with perseverance the race marked out for me. Are you up for that?

A PRAYER

Lord, I pray you stir us up as a people. That we will not lower our sights. We will lift our sights to you, towards that great 'Well done, good and faithful servant.' The only thing that's going to last is what's done for you, and we want to do great things for you because you're such a great and marvellous God. Help us to learn from your Word, be inspired by these great saints and go for it with everything we've got. Thank you, Jesus.

Amen.

1 CORINTHIANS 10:1-14

PAUL'S GREATEST HITS

1 CORINTHIANS 10:1-14

For I do not want you to be ignorant of the fact, brothers and sisters, that our ancestors were all under the cloud and that they all passed through the sea. They were all baptised into Moses in the cloud and in the sea. They all ate the same spiritual food and drank the same spiritual drink; for they drank from the spiritual rock that accompanied them, and that rock was Christ. Nevertheless, God was not pleased with most of them; their bodies were scattered in the wilderness.

Now these things occurred as examples to keep us from setting our hearts on evil things as they did. Do not be idolaters, as some of them were; as it is written: "The people sat down to eat and drink and got up to indulge in revelry." We should not commit sexual immorality, as some of them did – and in one day twenty-three thousand of them died. We should not test Christ, as some of them did – and were killed by snakes. And do not grumble, as some of them did – and were killed by the destroying angel.

These things happened to them as examples and were written down as warnings for us, on whom the culmination of the ages has come. So, if you think you are standing firm, be careful that you don't fall! No temptation has overtaken you except what is common to mankind. And God is faithful; he will not let you be tempted beyond what you can bear. But when you are tempted, he will also provide a way out so that you can endure it.

Therefore, my dear friends, flee from idolatry.

Corinth was a city dominated by idolatry. Everywhere you looked in Corinth, you'd see idols. The centre was a vast temple to the goddess Diana. Worshippers would be crying out day and night to the goddess of love and sex (there was no Tinder in Paul's day, just Aphrodite). If you were struggling with your health and you needed healing, you could cry out to Asklepieion, the god of healing and health. If you were a fisherman, as many were, you could call out to Poseidon, the god of the sea, to keep you safe and give you success in your business.

But like all false gods, however impressive they might have looked and sounded, crying out to any of them was ultimately going to end in disappointment. They were never going to be able to deliver what you really needed. Paul knew this, and because he knew his scriptures well, he knew that the first two of the ten commandments were about idolatry: 'You shall have no other gods before me' and 'you shall not make for yourself an image in the form of anything in heaven, above or on the earth beneath or in the waters below' (Deut 5:7-10). And while you might not immediately think Paul's words are relevant to us, trust me, they are super relevant. Martin Luther called the human heart 'an idol factory'. He also went on to say that if we get these first two commandments right, everything else will fall into place.

An idol is anything that takes the place of the true God in our hearts and affections. So we've made idols in our culture out of plenty of things. Yes, even Christian people make idols of things. It's so easy for a job or a career to become an idol. Providing for your family and all that goes with that is a brilliant thing. But if that becomes your obsession, if family life suffers, if you focus all your attention and all your passions on job and career, as so many do, it'll ultimately end up in destruction and disaster for you. Those things will never satisfy.

People even make good and beautiful things like marriage and loving relationships into idols. I know young men and women who have put the desire to be married – a good desire – before God. If I'm willing to sacrifice anything, even my relationship with God, to chase after a relationship, it becomes an idol and we end up in chaos. I know Christians who idolise their kids. It's a beautiful thing to bring up a child in a Christian family, but they worship their little ones and sacrifice so much for their sake to the point where they don't bring them up in line with the scriptures, putting God first.

And of course we live in a celebrity-obsessed culture. Recently Justin Bieber, perhaps the biggest pop star in the world, brought a gospel album out. There are some beautiful moments on the album and it certainly seems like he's on a journey towards Jesus. But Justin Bieber is famous for having 'beliebers' – millions and millions of young people who worship him. I remember hearing this hideous story about when Justin was going through chaos in his life and was taking drugs. Suddenly all these young girls were posting about self-harming unless he stopped taking drugs. How crazy is that? The worst thing for somebody is to be worshipped, when people are meant to worship the living God.

So why would you idolise any of those other things? Just like Aphrodite, Asklepieion and Poseidon, they're only going to lead to disappointment. They're never going to deliver what you really need. And ultimately, if we chase after things before God, Paul makes it clear that judgement will come. In the first part of 1 Corinthians 10 Paul sets out a clear warning from the history of God's people when they set their hearts on idols. 'What are you doing?', Paul asks them. How could you put anything before him?

Idolatry is perhaps the most dangerous and subtle temptation, but praise God, according to Paul, in one of his greatest hits, we don't have to give in to it. In one of his golden oldies, he says, 'If you think you're standing firm, be careful that you don't fall' (v12). Kind of a shot across the bow, isn't it, for those of us who think we're doing well in the faith? Paul says, be careful. Keep an eye on your life. Keep accountable. Keep in the Bible. Keep prayed up. Keep loving people and keep living a life of generosity, because you could fall, too.

I remember a time a few years ago, when a charismatic leader came over to plant a church here in Manchester, and lots of my friends and family were really impressed by him. He had a powerful ministry and lots of people were coming to Christ through it. But something was off. He started to say weird things like 'I can't remember the last time I sinned', or 'I really feel that I've reached a place where I've overcome sin – I'm not tempted the way I used to be.' And guess what happened? Soon after, it came out that he was involved in all sorts of sexual shenanigans. The church he planted fell apart and it was utter devastation.

In verse 13, Paul teaches that there are three things that can help us. We surely will be tempted but we don't need to give in. We don't need to give in to the sin that promises so much, but delivers so little. He writes, 'No temptation has overtaken you except what is common to mankind'. There's nothing, no area you're being tempted in, no matter how dark and dirty it feels, that isn't common to everyone. Satan has a very boring repertoire – he's coming to you with the same temptations he's going after people with all over the world. His primary temptation is to make us put things before God and make idols of other things except the living God.

Isn't it an amazing thought that Jesus has been tempted in every way that you are? There's no temptation that you've had that Jesus didn't have first. It says in Hebrews 4:15, 'We do not have a high priest who is unable to empathise with our weakness but we have one who's been tempted in every way, just as we are, yet did not sin.' That's our Jesus! Satan threw everything at him but Jesus conquered, Jesus overcame. He never gave in once to those temptations. And his Spirit is inside you to empower you, so you don't need to give in to temptation either. We don't have a distant God waving a big stick over us. We have a God who understands what it's like to be tempted in every way.

The second thing that it says is this: God won't let you be tempted beyond what you can bear. If you're facing a lot of temptation right now, it's because God knows you can handle it. He's trusting you to stand up under it. Even though sometimes temptation might feel almost unbearable, but we're not giving in because we've got our eyes on Jesus. He's number one in our lives. We're not going to give in to those things that maybe other people have given in to, and had to live with the consequences.

And the third wonderful thing that it says is this: that God will always provide a way out. He's faithful when you are tempted. He will also provide a way out so you can endure it. You don't have to take the way out, of course – we can choose our way and we can give into temptation – that choice is always there for us – but God promises he will provide a way out.

Paul finishes off this passage by saying, 'Therefore dear friends, flee from idolatry' (v14). Run a mile from putting anything before

Jesus. Jesus is life, and life to the full. The only way to squeeze the juice out of life is to have the Lord in his right place – he is the source of all joy and life and freedom and power. Why would you want to chase after anything else? Why would you want to put anything before him that can never deliver, can never satisfy?

A PRAYER

Jesus, we make you Lord once again – over our finances, over our relationships, over our sexuality, over all our desires. Lord, be number one. You deserve it. You gave everything for us and we give everything to you. We turn back to you. We put you in first place, Lord of all, boss of our lives. What you say goes. You're beautiful and wonderful.

Amen.

1 CORINTHIANS 10:14-31

PARTNERS IN THE FAMILY BUSINESS

*Therefore, my dear friends, flee from idolatry. I speak to sensible
people; judge for yourselves what I say. Is not the cup of thanksgiving
for which we give thanks a participation in the blood of Christ? And
is not the bread that we break a participation in the body of Christ?
Because there is one loaf, we, who are many, are one body, for we all
share the one loaf.*

*Consider the people of Israel: Do not those who eat the sacrifices
participate in the altar? Do I mean then that food sacrificed to an
idol is anything, or that an idol is anything? No, but the sacrifices of
pagans are offered to demons, not to God, and I do not want you to be
participants with demons. You cannot drink the cup of the Lord and
the cup of demons too; you cannot have a part in both the Lord's table
and the table of demons. Are we trying to arouse the Lord's jealousy?
Are we stronger than he?*

*"I have the right to do anything," you say – but not everything is
beneficial. "I have the right to do anything" – but not everything is
constructive. No one should seek their own good, but the good of
others. Eat anything sold in the meat market without raising questions
of conscience, for, "The earth is the Lord's, and everything in it."*

*If an unbeliever invites you to a meal and you want to go, eat
whatever is put before you without raising questions of conscience. But
if someone says to you, "This has been offered in sacrifice," then do
not eat it, both for the sake of the one who told you and for the sake of
conscience. I am referring to the other person's conscience, not yours.
For why is my freedom being judged by another's conscience? If I take
part in the meal with thankfulness, why am I denounced because of
something I thank God for?*

So whether you eat or drink or whatever you do, do it all for the glory of God.

. . . .

Simon Guillebaud recently told me about an Iranian Christian couple who'd managed to escape Iran and emigrate to the United States. It was their ticket to safety, to 'the land of the free', and they seized the opportunity with both hands. What was surprising though, was that after living in America for a while, the wife asked her husband to take her back to Iran. Listen to what she said: 'There is a satanic lullaby in this nation. All the Christians are asleep and I feel myself falling asleep, too.'

Here was a woman who'd escaped one of the very worst places to live as a Christian woman, where she faced daily dangers – loss of income and livelihood; separation from loved ones through incarceration; the very real probability of sexual violence, or worse. Yet she believed that the risk of all that was worth taking because of the greater danger to her soul through the insidious and deathly lies that she was being steadily drip-fed in the West.

Simon challenged me to think about it for a moment. Is she right? Is there really a 'satanic lullaby' playing in our land? Can you hear it? The song of consumerism, convenience, comfort, pleasure, personal satisfaction? Even the way we've done church? Are we being lulled to sleep?

As we come to this next part of Paul's letter, we hear a loud wake-up call. Paul wants his church to wake up and start living like the radical countercultural people God is calling them to be.

Interestingly, Paul draws their attention to holy communion, the meal that's at the centre of our Christian worship. Why is there a meal at the centre of the Christian faith? One reason for sure is because we need to be reminded often of what Jesus has done for us. As we remember the cross, how can we want to sin? Why would we want to conform to the pattern of this world? Why would we want to give into Satan's lullaby when Jesus died for us on the cross, when he gave everything so we could have new life? When he was punished for every sin I've ever committed, when he rose from the dead and conquered sin and death – why would we want to do that? When we drift away from the cross and Jesus' laid-down life, it suddenly becomes about us. Instead of taking up our cross daily we live a second-rate life.

Communion is meant to be the ultimate picture of our unity. The one thing we're all united around is the cross. We drink from one cup. We share one loaf. This holy meal, Paul says, is unlike any other. He says it is a participation in the death of Christ. We share in his death. If we fully understand the true meaning of communion, we see that it's a participation in our unity as the body of Christ. We come together, whether we're a billionaire or we live in the slums of Mumbai – wherever we're from, we are one body because we share in one bread and one cup. As we come to communion, we wake up to the fact that we're partners with Christ. We share in his death. We are partners with our chief partner Jesus in this glorious salvation business. And what a business it is!

Tesla is one of the big business success stories of the last decade. I'm told that if a few years ago you were lucky enough to have had £70,000, you could have bought a Tesla, the first electric car that Elon Musk brought into the world. If you'd done that, your Tesla would probably be worth about £20,000 today. But if instead of doing that, you'd invested £70,000 in Tesla shares, in other words, in the business itself, your £70,000 would now be worth £70 million. In other words, it would have been a pretty good investment.

Well, I can tell you about a far, far, far better investment than that. Investing in Jesus' kingdom business, investing in sacrificial living, investing in this upside-down gospel where you sow and you keep on sowing, means that before you know it, you'll be reaping a harvest all over the world. And the ripples go on into eternity! You never know what you're going to see when you just faithfully get on with it. Keep the cross central. Try to live in sweet relationship with others. Pray and serve and go and keep on going even when others give up. You keep on going and before you know it, look what Jesus has done. What an investment!

Paul says that we share in a 'cup of blessing' as we come together. Jewish people who heard his words would have known all about the third cup of the Passover meal which is called the cup of blessing. It was a reminder that they were blessed to be the children of God. They were blessed to be the people of Israel. They were blessed to have been led out of slavery into the promised land. We are so much more blessed in Christ in the new covenant. As we share in our meal, we are the ultimate blessed people, aren't we? We're blessed beyond blessed – we have, Paul said in Ephesians, 'every spiritual blessing in Christ in the heavenly realms' (1:3).

These blessings are not like blessings down here where they can come and go, and you can lose everything overnight. Who knows, Elon Musk might lose everything tomorrow. But I'm never going to lose my heavenly inheritance in Christ, because it's in the heavenly realms. I'm blessed with every spiritual blessing, and so are you and so is every person who's truly bowed the knee to Jesus.

Our very first Message prayer day was in a little side room at St Andrew's Church in Cheadle Hulme with Mark Pennells on his acoustic guitar and four or five of us there. I'll never forget it because I don't often get technicolour pictures from the Lord, but that day I did as we worshipped and prayed.

We were reading Ephesians 1, and as we were reflecting, I saw myself in a beautiful ornate mosaic hallway. In front of me were lots and lots of balconies with doorways. I asked the Lord what it was about and I felt him say, 'This is your spiritual inheritance in Christ. You're rejoicing in having every blessing, but you're just in the doorway! You're just in the reception area! Wait till you go through all those doors and one door leads to another door of blessing and one opportunity leads to another opportunity to serve the Lord and give Jesus glory!'

'One after another' – there really is so much more to come! This is the adventure of a lifetime and of eternity, to know every spiritual blessing in Christ!

And we share in the cup of blessing, Paul says, we share in a deep unity with our brothers and sisters. Paul wants to get a sense of the unity we have in Christ as brothers and sisters. If you know Jesus, there's a bond stronger than blood. Part of our ministry at the Message is to try and bring the church together with all its differences as one body to pray. There's never been a major move of God without united prayer. A single church, no matter how big it gets, can never do what we could all do together as the body of Christ.

The harvest is on – it's harvest time. It's time to open our eyes and wake up! Look at the opportunities before us – I really don't want to be lulled to sleep at a time like this.

A PRAYER

We look to you, Jesus, and we reflect again on
your cross and all it means. Help us to look to our
brothers and sisters, to look for the best in them
and cheer them on, to quickly forgive and come
together for this great purpose of sowing and
keep on sowing the good news of the gospel.

When we get to heaven, we want to have lived a first-
rate life, not a boring second-rate me-centred life,
but a big Jesus-filled life. Help us to live that life.

Amen.

1 CORINTHIANS 11:1-16

LET'S TALK ABOUT
PROBABLY THE
MOST CHALLENGING AND
CONTENTIOUS PASSAGE
IN THE WHOLE OF THE
NEW TESTAMENT

1 CORINTHIANS 11:1-16

I praise you for remembering me in everything and for holding to the traditions just as I passed them on to you. But I want you to realise that the head of every man is Christ, and the head of the woman is man, and the head of Christ is God. Every man who prays or prophesies with his head covered dishonours his head. But every woman who prays or prophesies with her head uncovered dishonours her head – it is the same as having her head shaved. For if a woman does not cover her head, she might as well have her hair cut off; but if it is a disgrace for a woman to have her hair cut off or her head shaved, then she should cover her head.

A man ought not to cover his head, since he is the image and glory of God; but woman is the glory of man. For man did not come from woman, but woman from man; neither was man created for woman, but woman for man. It is for this reason that a woman ought to have authority over her own head, because of the angels. Nevertheless, in the Lord woman is not independent of man, nor is man independent of woman. For as woman came from man, so also man is born of woman. But everything comes from God.

Judge for yourselves: Is it proper for a woman to pray to God with her head uncovered? Does not the very nature of things teach you that if a man has long hair, it is a disgrace to him, but that if a woman has long hair, it is her glory? For long hair is given to her as a covering. If anyone wants to be contentious about this, we have no other practice – nor do the churches of God.

This is probably the most contentious and controversial passage in the whole of the New Testament in our day and age. The best approach to looking at it is a hermeneutical approach. Now I'm not suggesting I'm some theologian or Bible scholar. I'm not, but I do love the Bible and want to study it And I don't want to bring my biases and my opinions to the Bible. I want to find out what is the word of God really saying here, to take Bible study seriously, with humility and sincerity, so that I'm better equipped to serve Jesus and hermeneutics is a good way of doing that.

Hermeneutics looks at three really important things when we come to a passage. The first thing is to look at the original language, because the Bible wasn't written in contemporary English, but ancient Hebrew and Greek. What did the words originally mean? The second thing we need to look at is the original context – in other words, the history and culture of the time. What was going on when the Bible writer wrote these things? And the third thing we need to look at is other scripture. God has given us a book with 66 different books within it – a library of books. We need to compare scripture with scripture if we're going to understand what God is really saying.

I don't want to bring to my teaching what Andy Hawthorne wishes it would say. I want to bring what I believe the Holy Spirit is saying through Paul to the church 2000 years ago, and what's relevant to us today. Thank God we have the Holy Spirit and his job is to lead us into all truth (John 16:13).

Paul says, 'I want you to realise that the head of every man is Christ, and the head of the woman is man, and the head of Christ is God' (v3). Sounds controversial. So let's get hermeneutical, baby!

What does the original language mean? Well, it means 'head', in the original Greek – it means the thing that sits on the top of your body. It can also mean, as lots of theologians have pointed out, a source, like the head of a river.

And what about other scriptures? What do all the scriptures say about men being 'head'? Well, there are lots of scriptures that say man in the home has spiritual authority and needs to take on a role of leadership. I believe I have a responsibility for spiritual leadership for my family. But in my family there is to be a functional subordination like that of Christ and God. Christ and God are perfectly equal, yet Jesus was willing to offer himself in love as a servant of the Father. If you read any of CS Lewis' writing about the Trinity, it's beautiful stuff. He calls it 'the great dance' and he's not talking about hip-hop, but where one person would defer to the other. Jesus defers to the Father and the Holy Spirit defers to Jesus – 'It's all about you, Jesus' – and Jesus defers to the Father in a beautiful unity and rhythm of love and blessing.

You can't get away from the passages in the New Testament talking about wives submitting to their husband and the classic one that upsets many women, and men I guess nowadays, is from Ephesians 5:

'Submit to one another out of reverence for Christ. Wives, submit yourselves to your own husbands as you do to the Lord. For the husband is the head of the wife as Christ is the head of the church, his body, of which he is the Saviour. Now as the church submits to Christ, so also wives should submit to their husbands in everything. Husbands, love your wives, just as Christ loved the church and gave himself up for her...' (verses 21-25).

There it is again. Same theme, just as Christ loves God and God loves Christ. Submit to one another out of reverence for Christ. It's the perfect picture of the way marriage is meant to work. I don't think many women would mind submitting to her husband who loves her the way Christ loved the church. If he totally has her best interest at heart, chooses the role of a servant, always promotes her.

Or we think again of Jesus in John 13 (see Chapter 7) where Jesus washed his disciples' feet. From that place of total security and headship, Jesus could take the perfect position of a servant.

We've been really inspired as a Message leadership team by the UK business Timpsons. They've got over 2,000 little shops on the high street. In a way, everything is wrong about Timpsons. They do shoe repairs – who has their shoes repaired these days when you can buy a pair of shoes for £10 from Primark? They do dry cleaning – when was the last time you had something dry cleaned? They even do photo printing – does anybody have photos printed anymore? And what's more, they love to employ ex-offenders. They've got about 600 of them working in their branches. It's hilarious to think that ex-offenders are cutting the keys to your car and your house. The business makes no sense, yet they make millions – they're a hugely successful business.

Their secret is service. Timpsons runs on 'upside-down' management. The whole ethos of the business is service. In other words, the higher you go, the lower you go. The chief executive's job is to serve the leadership team. The leadership team's job is to serve the regional managers, the regional managers' job is to serve the shop managers and the shop managers' job is to serve the customer. And if you go into Timpsons you can sniff it in the air. It makes no sense apart from they've got some serious kingdom culture going on.

Kingdom culture is service. Domineering and controlling has no place in marriage or in any other relationship in the kingdom. It's about service and mutual submission that makes Jesus look beautiful and does our best to cheer others on.

Then Paul carries on making life difficult after talking about headship, by talking about head coverings and haircuts. Again, context matters. The context is that in Corinth, married women had their heads covered as a sign they were married. If you had your hair down, it was a sign you were available to other men and in this crazy society where Pagan temples were basically mass orgies, it was not a good idea to come to church with your hair down. It was a provocative, even erotic thing to do. Cultures vary in what's acceptable and what's not. I remember going to a shopping centre in Namibia and seeing topless women walking around. It was fine there, but it wouldn't be appropriate for my church on a Sunday!

The question should be, what can you possibly do to point all the attention to Jesus to deflect everything to him? We need to think about everything we do through the lens of, 'Is there any chance it could hinder the spread of the gospel?' Maybe I have to give up my freedoms in order for that to happen. The key point is to prefer others in the way you worship.

Maybe we should be asking some tough questions of ourselves about whether the things we are wearing distract people's attention away from Jesus, and create divisions in the church. Is this a word to our bands and our cool funky musicians who go into schools in their costumes singing their great music and all the kids are screaming at them in a mosh pit and wanting their autographs at the end of their gigs? What can they possibly do to point all the attention to Jesus, to deflect everything to him? Because it's bad for your soul and dishonours God as soon as it starts to become about you and not about him.

How about all the religious garb that some Christian leaders wear? Clothing that seems to give the impression that there's a qualitative difference between them and us – whether that's clerical robes or funky designer trainers. Maybe that's not helping people. Paul would say ditch anything that would hinder the gospel.

What would it look like today to truly serve – to take the place of a servant, not so others can see? It's not about the chief executive making the tea for the whole office so that everyone's impressed. But kind, generous, behind-the-scenes acts of service. What would that look like for you if you've got any leadership responsibility – what would Jesus-style servant leadership look like in your context?

But also, what can I do to serve my spouse in love? What can I do to make sure the way I worship is all about Jesus and not about me? And then, finally: how can I be truly diligent in my study of the Bible, come to it with an open, servant-hearted, humble approach so I can mine the gold that's in the Word of God that will change my life?

....

A PRAYER

Lord, help us to emulate Jesus, 'who, being in very nature
God, did not consider equality with God something to
be used to his own advantage; rather, he made himself
nothing by taking the very nature of a servant, being
made in human likeness. And being found in appearance
as a man, he humbled himself by becoming obedient
to death – even death on a cross!' (Phil 2:6-8).

Amen.

....

1 CORINTHIANS 11:17-33

HOW TO DO MORE HARM THAN GOOD

1 CORINTHIANS 11:17-33

*In the following directives I have no praise for you, for your meetings
do more harm than good. In the first place, I hear that when you come
together as a church, there are divisions among you, and to some extent
I believe it. No doubt there have to be differences among you to show
which of you have God's approval. So then, when you come together,
it is not the Lord's Supper you eat, for when you are eating, some of
you go ahead with your own private suppers. As a result, one person
remains hungry and another gets drunk. Don't you have homes to eat
and drink in? Or do you despise the church of God by humiliating
those who have nothing? What shall I say to you? Shall I praise you?
Certainly not in this matter!*

*For I received from the Lord what I also passed on to you: The Lord
Jesus, on the night he was betrayed, took bread, and when he had given
thanks, he broke it and said, "This is my body, which is for you; do this
in remembrance of me." In the same way, after supper he took the cup,
saying, "This cup is the new covenant in my blood; do this, whenever
you drink it, in remembrance of me." For whenever you eat this bread
and drink this cup, you proclaim the Lord's death until he comes.*

*So then, whoever eats the bread or drinks the cup of the Lord in an
unworthy manner will be guilty of sinning against the body and blood
of the Lord. Everyone ought to examine themselves before they eat of
the bread and drink from the cup. For those who eat and drink without
discerning the body of Christ eat and drink judgement on themselves.
That is why many among you are weak and sick, and a number of
you have fallen asleep. But if we were more discerning with regard to
ourselves, we would not come under such judgment. Nevertheless,
when we are judged in this way by the Lord, we are being disciplined so
that we will not be finally condemned with the world.*

So then, my brothers and sisters, when you gather to eat, you should all eat together. Anyone who is hungry should eat something at home, so that when you meet together it may not result in judgement.

And when I come I will give further directions.

. . . .

I don't know if The Message could have survived for the last 30 years without our prayer days – where we gather in the Lord's presence, repenting, pressing into worship and stirring one another up. It was really hard during the pandemic not being able to gather in person as a team, to sing our hearts out, hear amazing testimonies and teaching, and pour out our prayers to God. They are such precious times.

So I can't imagine how it would feel if, after visiting one of our prayer days, a godly leader wrote to me and said, 'Andy, your meetings are officially doing more harm than good.' How hurt I would feel, as the ripples went out into our leadership team! But that is exactly what happened 2000 years ago. The Corinthians thought they were having a whale of a time in the Lord's presence. And yet Paul said 'in the following, I have no praise for you, for your meetings do more harm than good … When you come together, it's not the Lord's supper you eat' (17).

So here's the big question: could it actually be that we as a church are doing a similar thing in our day? Could it be that we're giving in to the spirit of the age in the way the Corinthians were 2,000 years ago?

At the worship gatherings of the early church, communion was always central – it was a meal, a banquet, a party instituted by Jesus before his death. The Lord had told them to do it, and they were obeying. I love the fact that Jesus was a party person – he loved to eat and drink with his friends. In fact that's exactly what the Pharisees condemned him for in Mark 2:16, 'He eats and drinks with tax collectors and sinners.' What they called a bad thing was actually a beautiful thing – Jesus wanted to spend his time in an intimate fellowship with people. In those days, table fellowship was super important – it was where you developed relationships, where you shared your life. But you tended to do it just with your own circle, in your own class or culture, and Jesus trampled all over that.

Don't you love the invitation in Revelation 3:20, 'Here I am! I stand at the door and knock. If anyone hears my voice and opens the door, I will come in and eat with that person and they with me'? We often make it an evangelistic verse and I guess it could be. But I think primarily it's a verse for us as Christian disciples. Jesus is saying, 'I'm knocking on the door of your heart. I want to come in. And I want to share my secrets with you and yours with me and I want to develop a relationship as a picture of the great banquet to come.'

Jesus is preparing a banquet for me and you. He's preparing a place. As if I deserve to be at that great banquet on the final day – as if you do! But there's stuff he's preparing that no eye has seen, no ear has heard (1 Cor 2:9). The stories we're going to hear, the food we're going to eat, the drink we're going to enjoy on that great day... Are you looking forward to it? That's a great invitation and he's knocking on the door of our hearts today and saying, 'Come on, open the door, open your heart, spend time with me, and you'll get a little taste, a little down payment of that banquet now.'

Jesus would have enjoyed eating and drinking with his ragtag bunch of disciples in so many different places and at so many different times. And yet, the night before he was betrayed, Jesus proceeded with the ultimate Passover meal, a special meal to tell again the story of the escape from Egypt, of being rescued, using the lamb and the bitter herbs and the wine as symbols. But then Jesus went off-script (Jesus was allowed to do what nobody else who ever lived could do). Now he said, 'This is my body, which is for you... this cup is the cup of the new covenant in my blood' (v25). Yes, you've had the Passover, being rescued from certain death and judgement by the blood of a lamb, but this is a new thing.

This speaks to me of two things. When we come together with the cross at the centre, with Jesus at the centre, his presence is very real. 'This is my body. This is my blood shed for you.' It speaks of his presence, doesn't it? Jesus is very present, what a holy thing! But it also speaks to me of Jesus being absent. 'Do this until I come.' Jesus is present with us now, but there's so much more to come. We share a meal together now, looking for the great banquet that we'll share with Jesus in the future.

I love that Paul adds, 'For whenever you eat this bread and drink this cup, you proclaim the Lord's death until he comes' (v26). That's our job – to proclaim the cross and the resurrection until he comes. I've told my trustees at the Message to sack me if I ever take money off anybody if it means we're not allowed to proclaim the Lord's death and resurrection. If we can't proclaim the gospel, we're not interested. Yes, we want to do good works, we want to serve people, of course we do. But I also want to know the best news is going to be told to them – the news of the death and the resurrection and the soon return of Jesus. Until he comes, somebody's got to keep proclaiming that gospel and we've been given the baton for our generation.

I don't know when he's coming, I just know it's going to be soon. Maybe it's another thousand years. Maybe it's going to be tomorrow, I don't know. What I do know is what I want to be doing when Jesus returns – I want to be proclaiming the death and resurrection of Jesus. I don't want to be arguing with my wife when Jesus returns like a thief in the night! I don't want to be falling out with a fellow believer! I don't want to be watching something dodgy on the internet when the thief in the night returns! When Jesus returns, I want to be found either proclaiming his death with genuine believers who were surrendering all in true cross-centred worship, or I want to be out there in the world relevantly proclaiming the good news. That's our charge – that's what we've been called to do.

The problem with the church at Corinth is that they'd moved away from true holy communion into a disorderly gathering where people brought their own food. The richer ones knew that Jesus was a party person so they brought the good stuff to the gathering – they brought the equivalent of fine champagne and bordeaux red and smoked salmon, and canapés – sounds like fun, doesn't it? But it's not fun if they're in the same gathering as poor people who can hardly afford sandwiches or a bottle of water. Holy communion should speak of 'common union', and yet they were divided into rich and poor. The very thing that was meant to unite them, divided them. Paul calls it wrong, that it's doing more harm than good.

I hope you agree that verse 21 is a bit of a shocker – 'Some of you when you come together, you don't even wait for others. You just eat and drink and some of you even get drunk.' Which is worse in the church? Hungry and poor people watching while others gorged themselves, or getting drunk? I think they have equal weight in this scripture. Just like Ephesians 5:18 has equal weight: 'Don't get drunk on wine, which leads to debauchery. Instead, be filled with the Spirit.' It's a dual command. Don't get drunk in church, but whatever you do, don't forget the poor. Don't just get on with your comfortable life and forget the poor. Don't get drunk with wine because it leads to debauchery. Instead, be filled with the Spirit! It's a command. In the past perhaps we've got hot under the collar in the church about not getting drunk. But at the same time we've forgotten the poor. We know getting drunk can lead to debauchery, but not being filled with the Spirit can lead to even greater debauchery. It's a command that we are filled with the Spirit today. Because if I truly am, I'll never want to go in any other direction.

....

A PRAYER

Holy Spirit, examine our hearts. Are there any factions and divisions there with other believers? Have we allowed stuff to carry on that needs dealing with? Help us to forgive people quickly, to build bridges with others.

Have we got on with our greedy life in the richest generation in history and forgotten the poor? Have we been gorging in the West while so many in the developing world are starving right now? We repent of that.

Have we let our passion to proclaim the cross in season and out of season wane at all? We're sorry, Lord, that we forget. I pray, Lord, you'll bring conviction in those areas.

Jesus, you're knocking on the door of our heart, so we open our hearts to you – come in, Jesus. Share your secrets with us, share what's on your heart and we'll obey.

Amen.

....

1 CORINTHIANS 12:1-11

YOUR SPIRITUAL GIFTS AND HOW TO USE THEM

Now about the gifts of the Spirit, brothers and sisters, I do not want you to be uninformed. You know that when you were pagans, somehow or other you were influenced and led astray to mute idols. Therefore I want you to know that no one who is speaking by the Spirit of God says, "Jesus be cursed," and no one can say, "Jesus is Lord," except by the Holy Spirit.

There are different kinds of gifts, but the same Spirit distributes them. There are different kinds of service, but the same Lord. There are different kinds of working, but in all of them and in everyone it is the same God at work.

Now to each one the manifestation of the Spirit is given for the common good. To one there is given through the Spirit a message of wisdom, to another a message of knowledge by means of the same Spirit, to another faith by the same Spirit, to another gifts of healing by that one Spirit, to another miraculous powers, to another prophecy, to another distinguishing between spirits, to another speaking in different kinds of tongues, and to still another the interpretation of tongues. All these are the work of one and the same Spirit, and he distributes them to each one, just as he determines.

Here's something we all need to remember: Satan is a copycat. He really is boring, he just copies. God is the God of 'See, I'm doing a new thing' (Is 43:19) – he's full of new life, imagination and creativity. But Satan is a copycat and longs to copy every spiritual gift in a twisted way. Recently I was listening to a voodoo high priest on BBC Radio 4 talking about all the weird manifestations and all the strange things that can happen and some of the healing he's able to do. There is certainly crazy stuff going on around voodoo but it's all a fake satanic copycat of the real thing.

Paul's readers, the church in Corinth, would have had similar kinds of spiritual experience. They were largely new believers who had been saved from a pagan culture, and lives of pagan worship. Paul says 'You know what it was to be moved by mute idols' (v2). He talks about them being 'led astray'. And then he goes on to say, 'but I don't want you to be uninformed about real spirituality – about God's spiritual gifts'. The word he uses for uninformed is ignorant – 'I don't want you to be an ignoramus when it comes to spiritual gifts.'

There are powers of dark and light all around us, and sadly many Christians are ignoramuses in this area. There's a whole spiritual realm out there – powers of good and evil. Ephesians 6:12 says, 'Our struggle is not against flesh and blood, but against the rulers, against the authorities, against the powers of this dark world, against the spiritual forces of evil in the heavenly realm.' Our battle isn't primarily with people. It's with the whole spiritual forces of darkness in the heavenly realms, and it's mighty important we put on the full armour of God, pray in the Spirit, move in the power of the Holy Spirit and exercise the gifts God has given us for the breaking down of strongholds (2 Cor 10:4).

But also he also didn't want the Corinthians to become so obsessed with the supernatural – and this happens – that they weren't obsessed enough with Jesus. The supernatural will only truly flow as we get obsessed with the giver of the gift, not the gift itself. That's why he says in verse 3, 'I want you to know that no one who is speaking by the Spirit of God says, "Jesus be cursed," and no one can say, "Jesus is Lord," except by the Holy Spirit.'

Maybe there was some concern when the Corinthian believers went off speaking in tongues. Pagan religions have mysterious languages or tongues, too. Satan is a copycat, so maybe they experienced tongues in their pagan religion. Perhaps they were asking, 'How do we know these people who are now speaking in tongues in the power of the Spirit are not cursing Jesus?' So Paul says, 'No one filled with the Spirit can say "Jesus be cursed"' (v3).

In Paul's day in Corinth, it was a revolutionary, countercultural, super dangerous thing to say 'Jesus is Lord' because they knew Caesar was Lord – there were monuments to Caesar that people had to bow down to all throughout the empire, Caesar is Lord. Paul says, no, Jesus is Lord. The Spirit will show you who's truly Lord.

The key verse in this whole passage is verse 7 – 'Now to each one the manifestation of the Spirit is given for the common good.' Here are four things I believe God would say to us as we seek to manifest the spiritual gifts that God has given us for the good of his world and for the glory of Jesus.

The first thing God wants us to know from this passage is the Spirit is given to every Christian. Literally, the word 'given' in the Greek means a 'birthday gift'. When you become a Christian, you receive the most precious birthday gift in the world. The Holy Spirit in your heart, Jesus comes into your life. It's a love gift from the Father. The Bible calls it the deposit guaranteeing your inheritance. I'm going to see Jesus face to face. I'm going to get welcomed into heaven. I don't deserve it, but I know because the Holy Spirit is in my heart – I've got that deposit guaranteeing my inheritance, and so has every Christian. The Holy Spirit is given to each one. Today, if you don't have the Holy Spirit in your life, receive Christ, make him Lord, and you will receive the most precious gift in the world: the forgiveness of your sins and the confidence by the power of his Spirit that you're going to join me in heaven.

The second thing that Paul says is that he's the Spirit of the living God and that means he's behind all the gifts. We are different in our gifts and ministries. Even in our effectiveness, we're different, but they're all from him and he decides who gets what for the furthering of his purposes.

Personally I'd love to be more musical – I feel jealous when I see the amazing musicians at The Message. I'd love to be more pastoral, but I know I'm not a great pastor. I'd love to have all the gifts in the full measure, but God says, 'No, for you, Andy, this is what I'm giving you because this is your part to play in my purposes.' Do you know what your spiritual gifts are? Well, read the spiritual gifts in 1 Corinthians 10. Look at other passages like Ephesians 4 and Romans 12. There are at least 18 specific supernatural gifts of the Spirit and you need to know what yours are. If you don't know, seek the Lord on it, and talk to your Christian friends and leaders. Then work out a way to share them in the most servant-hearted, humble way possible and see what God does.

The third thing Paul says is, the gifts are to manifest the Spirit. Don Carson wrote a book about these chapters called 'Showing the Spirit.' That's our job in a nutshell – we're meant to be people who show the world the Holy Spirit. Jesus didn't just say 'I'm the light of the world.' Of course he is! He went on to say, 'You are the light of the world' (Matthew 5:14). How could we be the light of the world? The answer is by the Spirit within. And he went on to say, you don't put a bowl over the light – you've got to put it on a stand and it will extinguish the deepest darkness in the world by the power of the Spirit. It's impossible to get away from the fact as you read the New Testament, that the church of Jesus is meant to be a thoroughly supernatural thing. We're meant to live lives that can be explained in no other way than by the power of the Spirit within.

Trying to do God's work in our own strength is exhausting. But we're not meant to be doing it in our own strength! We're meant to be doing it with the power of the Spirit within. Did you ever hear about the mouse and the elephant who walked across the bridge? When they got to the other side, the mouse said, 'Wow, we made that bridge shake, didn't we?' That's like us, isn't it? We'll get to the other side and we'll be saying, 'We sure made society shake, didn't we?' But we brought transformation only because we had the huge, great elephant of the Holy Spirit behind us. We were just the little mouse.

The final thing that Paul says in this verse is that the Spirit is given for the common good. Not just so we can have the 'thrill of the fill' as someone once put it, but so everybody around us can be blessed. As William Booth said, this is all about 'others.'

It's easy in our self-centred, self-obsessed society to approach church or a ministry like The Message as an arena to demonstrate our own talents. But this is not a stage on which to perform. It's a place to give glory to Jesus and point to him. It's a place of 'service', Paul says in verse 5. The more filled you are, the more you're moving in the supernatural gifts of the Holy Spirit, the more you'll want to serve, to work in his strength for the common good.

Our ministry is ultimately a platform to point to Jesus and see him get the reward he deserves. The Holy Spirit always points to Jesus. If you're filled with the Holy Spirit, a sure sign is you will be pointing to Jesus. You'll do everything you can to see he gets the glory. The more we realise that, the more the gifts will flow and the more the world will be blessed.

....

A PRAYER

Jesus, you said a wonderful thing in Luke 11. You said, 'If
you sinful people know how to give good gifts to your
children, how much more will your Heavenly Father
give the Holy Spirit to those who ask him?' (v13).

We pray, Lord, that you'll fill us with your Spirit. Give us
those beautiful gifts and help us to serve well in them.
Help us to do your work your way. Come, Holy Spirit.

Amen.

....

1 CORINTHIANS 12:12-31

THE BODY BEAUTIFUL

Just as a body, though one, has many parts, but all its many parts form one body, so it is with Christ. For we were all baptised by one Spirit so as to form one body – whether Jews or Gentiles, slave or free – and we were all given the one Spirit to drink. Even so the body is not made up of one part but of many.

Now if the foot should say, "Because I am not a hand, I do not belong to the body," it would not for that reason stop being part of the body. And if the ear should say, "Because I am not an eye, I do not belong to the body," it would not for that reason stop being part of the body. If the whole body were an eye, where would the sense of hearing be? If the whole body were an ear, where would the sense of smell be? But in fact God has placed the parts in the body, every one of them, just as he wanted them to be. If they were all one part, where would the body be? As it is, there are many parts, but one body.

The eye cannot say to the hand, "I don't need you!" And the head cannot say to the feet, "I don't need you!" On the contrary, those parts of the body that seem to be weaker are indispensable, and the parts that we think are less honourable we treat with special honour. And the parts that are unpresentable are treated with special modesty, while our presentable parts need no special treatment. But God has put the body together, giving greater honour to the parts that lacked it, so that there should be no division in the body, but that its parts should have equal concern for each other. If one part suffers, every part suffers with it; if one part is honoured, every part rejoices with it.

Now you are the body of Christ, and each one of you is a part of it. And God has placed in the church first of all apostles, second prophets, third teachers, then miracles, then gifts of healing, of helping, of guidance, and of different kinds of tongues. Are all apostles? Are all prophets? Are all teachers? Do all work miracles? Do all have gifts of healing? Do all speak in tongues? Do all interpret? Now eagerly desire the greater gifts.

The human body is an amazing thing. You've got around 30 trillion cells in your body that are constantly reproducing. Did you know that? 30 trillion – not 30 million, not 30 billion, 30 trillion! All of them have your unique DNA and all of them make up you. In the last second alone you produced 25 million cells. In the next year you'll shed roughly the weight of your human body in cells, you dirty beast!

You're amazing, you're incredible. You're unique. There's never been another you – God made you and threw away the mould. You're designed by the living God with the greatest care, and with that comes the opportunity to demonstrate Jesus in all his beauty and all his splendour.

As Paul moves on with his teaching for the church, he uses the analogy of the body to describe the beautiful unity and diversity that we're meant to experience. There's nothing like the church at its best – a beautiful mixture of every culture and colour all working together. One of my favourite verses in the New Testament is Ephesians 2:10. It says this: 'You are God's workmanship' – literally 'You are God's masterpiece.' You're a masterpiece, God's masterpiece, created in Christ Jesus to do good works which he planned in advance for us to do. Yours are different to mine, but the world needs to see them all worked out.

Paul says if we're going to be that kind of church, we need to know three things and we need to let them sink in and then live them out. The first thing we need to know is that we need each other – 'Now if the foot should say, "Because I am not a hand, I do not belong to the body," it would not for that reason stop being part of the body. And if the ear should say, "Because I am not an eye, I do not belong to the body," it would not for that reason stop being part of the body' (verses 15-16).

I need you, and you need me. I need you to fulfil my calling in Jesus and you need me to fulfil yours, and we need to work together. Do you know how to stop the flow of the Holy Spirit, to stop what God wants to do on the earth? Go about with an independent spirit which says, 'It's all about me and I've got to work it out and I've got to do all the jobs.'

I really don't want to upset my ordained friends but the more I think about ordination, the more I think in many ways it's a bit crazy. Especially if it gives the impression that one man or woman has to stand at the front and have all the gifts while the people line themselves up in pews just listening. It's like an ugly picture of an oversized mouth. Forget Mick Jagger's mouth – here's the big mouth at the front of church who's got to do all the teaching and all the talking and all the leadership. Or the idea that one person should do all the pastoral care? Like one great big oversized ear, doing all the listening? Here's the pastor trying to do all the pastoral care by themselves, burning themselves out trying to do the work of the whole body.

No, the church of Jesus is meant to be all parts working together, and leadership is all about releasing others into the works of service. We all ought to work together for the glory of Jesus, recognising we need each other, helping each other to reach our potential in Jesus. That's the call.

The second thing Paul wants us to know is we're all different: 'If the whole body were an eye, where would the sense of hearing be? If the whole body were an ear, where would the sense of smell be? But in fact God has placed the parts in the body, every one of them, just as he wanted them to be. If they were all one part, where would the body be? As it is, there are many parts, but one body' (verses 17-20).

Let's rejoice in that! God really did throw away the mould when he made you. Let's learn to relish our differences rather than be threatened by others' differences. David Pryor said this: 'The community which is alive to the Spirit is committed by scripture to the costly struggle of living out the reconciliation of all men, to one another unto God by uniting black and white, intellectual and action-orientated businessmen, new believer and mature disciple, Jew and Gentile, young and old, male and female, single and married.'

We need to be committed to working out what this looks like. All our diversity, all our differences makes for a church that's irresistible to a world in need. A church that values each other, a church that cheers each other on.

The third and final thing Paul wants us to know from these verses is that we really need to care for each other: 'Those parts of the body that seem to be weaker are indispensable, and the parts that we think are less honourable we treat with special honour. And the parts that are unpresentable are treated with special modesty, while our presentable parts need no special treatment. But God has put the body together, giving greater honour to the parts that lacked it, so that there should be no division in the body' (verses 22-25).

A church that works like a body and manifests Jesus cares for every part of itself. If I smack my thumb with a hammer, it is not just my thumb that hurts, my whole body knows about it! We need a church that gives special care to the weaker brothers; God has put the body together, giving greater honour to the parts that lacked it. We need, in church and in our lives, to be looking out for weaker brothers, people who may feel useless, but most certainly aren't. We give special care to weaker brothers and sisters who may feel hidden away and dispensable. One of the most beautiful things you ever can see is people who've come to Jesus feeling like that, feeling broken, feeling hopeless and they bloom like a flower. We've seen it. It's the most precious thing in the world, isn't it? Suddenly they're alive.

Paul says we need a church which weeps with those who weeps and rejoices with those who rejoice (Rom 12:15). I'm embarrassed to say this, but I find it easier to weep with those who weep than to rejoice with those who rejoice. I find it easy to weep with people who are hurting and broken and are having a bad deal out of life. But what about people who seem like they're getting a better deal out of life, when I think I deserve that blessing? What about if we could just rejoice any time blessing flows into the body of Christ?

There's only one body – it's not just The Message, it's not just your church. It's the whole beautiful, worldwide, multicoloured, unique, amazing body of Jesus – the church of Jesus. Let's represent him well. What would it look like if you thought every moment today, 'I want people to see Jesus in me. I want to manifest him in all his beauty and all his kindness, in all his forgiveness and all his servant-heartedness.'

You can never do that on your own. But by the power of the Spirit within, you can play your part and we can together let people see what Jesus is like. And that's what's going to change the world.

A PRAYER

Thank you, Jesus, that we all drink of the one Spirit, and we receive you afresh today. And we ask, Lord, more than ever, that we will live up to that high calling to be people who are not just named 'Christian' but who live up to it.

Send us out today to be different for you, to be radical for you, to be everything you want us to be, by the power of your Spirit. What a privilege to be part of your body on earth! Thank you, Jesus.

Amen.

1 CORINTHIANS 13:1-7

WHAT LOVE IS AND WHAT LOVE AIN'T

1 CORINTHIANS 13:1-7

If I speak in the tongues of men or of angels, but do not have love, I am only a resounding gong or a clanging cymbal. If I have the gift of prophecy and can fathom all mysteries and all knowledge, and if I have a faith that can move mountains, but do not have love, I am nothing. If I give all I possess to the poor and give over my body to hardship that I may boast, but do not have love, I gain nothing.

Love is patient, love is kind. It does not envy, it does not boast, it is not proud. It does not dishonour others, it is not self-seeking, it is not easily angered, it keeps no record of wrongs. Love does not delight in evil but rejoices with the truth. It always protects, always trusts, always hopes, always perseveres.

Today around the world there will be thousands, maybe tens of thousands, of Christian weddings, and many will read this chapter as part of their marriage service. It contains some of the most famous words about love ever written. Imagine if Paul were still around today getting royalties – he'd be a wealthy guy! But it's not really a passage written for weddings at all. It's a passage written for a church in turmoil.

In Chapter 13 of 1 Corinthians, Paul is continuing to respond to the way the church at Corinth are behaving. He wants them to understand what it looks like not just to move in the gifts of the Spirit, but to live the life of the Spirit.

It's been said you can replace the word 'love' in this chapter with the name of Jesus: Jesus is patient. Jesus is kind. Jesus does not envy. Jesus does not boast Jesus is not proud. Jesus does not dishonour others. Jesus is not self-seeking. Jesus is not easily angered. Jesus keeps no record of wrong. He does not delight in evil but rejoices with the truth. He always protects, always trusts, always hopes, always perseveres.

Isn't Jesus ace? He's wonderful. But then I had a little thought... how about replacing it with my name? Andy's patient, Andy's kind, Andy doesn't envy, Andy doesn't boast. Andy's not proud, Andy doesn't dishonour others, Andy isn't self-seeking. Andy's not easily angered, and he keeps no record of wrong and he doesn't delight in evil but rejoices with the truth. Andy always protects, always trusts, always hopes, always perseveres...

I don't quite live up to the mark. How about you? I want to be more like Jesus and it's only by the power of the Spirit that this can happen. We can manifest the love of Jesus as we press in and come to his Word more and more, and unless we are actually becoming more like Jesus in his great love, there's something deeply wrong.

First Corinthians 13 must be read in context – it's not meant to be read as a lovely poem, one chapter in isolation. It's meant to be understood in the context of a church that was falling way short. Can you believe this church in Corinth was bursting with gifts, yet they weren't just falling out, there were lawsuits amongst believers? Can you believe that there was a church where some were feasting whilst the poor in the church went hungry? They were. And so are we.

Paul's words in chapter 12 put it in context – this was a gifted church, an amazing church, but Paul wanted them to realise that the greatest gifts in the world literally mean nothing, zip, zilch, without love. The greatest Christian vision in the world means nothing without love, including ours. Our schools work, community groceries, Eden projects, Advance, Festival Manchester... none of it means anything without love.

Here's how strongly Paul makes his point: Imagine a businessman who becomes a Christian then starts to have some success. He tithes and as he tithes, his business becomes even more successful. So he gears up his giving and before he knows it, he's giving 20% of his vast wealth away. Then he gets to the stage where his heart feels broken towards the poor and the hungry, and so he gives even more. Finally he decides to give it all away – he sells everything, his houses, his cars, his businesses, and gives all the money to feed the poor.

Or imagine a young couple in the church, young missionaries sent out to the mission field. They go to a hostile environment to preach the gospel and tragically the local militia attack their home and the whole family is burnt to death as martyrs.

We would surely celebrate these people – the generous businessman, the missionaries – as heroes. But you know what Paul says? 'If I give all I possess to the poor and give over my body to hardship that I may boast, but do not have love, I gain nothing' (v3). They're challenging words, aren't they? None of it means anything without love. So we'd better test ourselves, hadn't we?

I test a lot of things at The Message as chief executive. I test the prayer temperature regularly – I want to know, are we stepping up in prayer? Are we growing in the discipline of prayer? Are we praying harder, longer, more passionately? Are we fasting and praying? I'll test salvations. I want to know about how the mission's going. I want to hear the stories. I want to know how many people are coming to Christ. You count what counts, don't you? I test the regular giving to The Message. I get reports every month. I want to know how many people are signing up for small regular gifts because it really matters to me. I don't just want to rely on a few wealthy businesspeople to fund this thing. We need thousands of people who own the vision and join in. I test all those things.

But as I read Paul's words, I ask myself, how often do I test the 'love temperature' at The Message? How good are we at loving and forgiving and serving and blessing? And are we growing in that area, because without that, you can forget the rest of it, says Paul.

The word used for 'love' in this passage is one that was rarely used in New Testament times. There were four words for 'love' in ancient Greek and the word used here is *'agape'*, a word that was hardly ever used in early church times. It's almost like they needed a new word to describe the amazing, undeserved love of Jesus, which was defined particularly by love for unworthy people like us. Jesus' love is defined by his love for those who don't deserve to be loved.

I am thrilled with what's been happening with our community groceries, as people turn up, often very broken, struggling with debt and crippled by all sorts of issues in their life, and they experience a bunch of people who love them. We don't just feed them – we share with them the love of Jesus. We have a whole programme across the UK called 'Love where you live.' And it's about demonstrating the love of Jesus, cleaning up streets, finding the people whose houses are in greatest need of help, offering tender loving care and blessing them, no questions asked. I love that and I want us to grow in those areas of the ministry. I pray that there'll be a day where people know that when the Christians turn up, good things are going to happen.

Mother Teresa seemed to have cracked this better than most. She was remarkable. You know what her famous last words were? She said, 'I love you, Jesus' as she died and went to heaven. Apparently she kept saying it repeatedly, 'I love you Jesus, I love you Jesus, I love you Jesus.' Wouldn't you like those to be your last words? And I guess she learned to love the poor and the broken and the marginalised and the hurting and sacrificed so much because first she loved Jesus. We need to love him and be consumed and obsessed with him so we can love the world in his name.

From verses 1 to 7, Paul wants us to know two things. First is that Christian community without love is actually worse than nothing. In Chapter 8, he has already said that 'knowledge puffs up, but love builds up' (v1) and it is very easy to get puffed up. How easy it is to get into a competitive spirit between ministries and churches. It's a horrible thing when churches are competing for people and profile and finance, or jostling for position. It stinks and it's wrong, and it's not of God. It's not about having the best visuals or the best songs or the best kids' and youth work. Of course we want to do things with excellence, but without love, Paul says, it's not just no good, it's doing more harm than good.

I actually think the greatest hindrance to revival is Christians' lack of love. There are so many prodigals out there – I meet them all the time – who still love God but hate his church because they've been repelled by a lack of love. Is that tragic or what? Even if we could just mobilise that army we'd transform the nation! Paul actually says that without love, I gain nothing, but he goes further even than that – he says without love I *am* nothing (v2).

So the second thing Paul wants us to know is what love is and what love does. Read those words again. Let them sink in. Allow yourself to feel a little bit convicted. I know I am....

'Love is patient. Love is kind. Love does not envy, it does not boast, it's not proud. Doesn't dishonour others. It's not self seeking. It's not easily angered. It keeps no record of wrongs. Love does not delight in evil but rejoices with the truth. It always protects. Always trusts, always hopes and always perseveres.'

He wants them to know that a truly loving person will do some stuff and not do other stuff. The words Paul uses here are present tense words – in other words, these things have to be worked out. There are some people who've got there – they've got to that place where they habitually love others, it's so ingrained, they've practised it for so long, like a growing muscle they've developed by constant use, constantly loving even in the face of other people not loving them.

In Colossians 3:14, Paul tells another church to 'put on love.' Sometimes we Christians have to put on love – to make it an active decision. I make the conscious choice to 'put on love' and then guess what, God makes it become real. He says, 'Put on love because it binds all the other virtues together.' There's a glue of love, compassion and kindness, and the sweetness of Jesus holds all the other virtues together.

Jesus said in John 13, 'A new command I give you: love one another as I have loved you. So you must love one another. And by this everyone will know you're my disciples' (v34). The greatest evangelistic tool is right there: love one another. As we pour out hearts of love, everyone's going to know he's Lord.

··

A PRAYER

We pray, Lord, that conviction will come
now, leading to genuine repentance from
our self-centeredness and lack of love.

Jesus, we want to be more like you. Help
us get off our silly little agendas and get on
to your agenda of loving the world.

Amen.

··

1 CORINTHIANS 13:8-13

LOVE THAT LASTS FOREVER

1 CORINTHIANS 13:8-13

Love never fails. But where there are prophecies, they will cease; where there are tongues, they will be stilled; where there is knowledge, it will pass away. For we know in part and we prophesy in part, but when completeness comes, what is in part disappears. When I was a child, I talked like a child, I thought like a child, I reasoned like a child. When I became a man, I put the ways of childhood behind me. For now we see only a reflection as in a mirror; then we shall see face to face. Now I know in part; then I shall know fully, even as I am fully known.

And now these three remain: faith, hope and love. But the greatest of these is love.

We use the word 'love' so tritely and so lightly these days. But in this passage, as in the one just before it, Paul uses a word which eloquently and beautifully describes divine love: it is a love that 'never fails.'

Human love is going to fail us time and again but God's love never fails. That is my testimony – God's love has never failed me. I've regularly failed God, but God's love has never failed me.

These Corinthians thought they were so special because of their knowledge and amazing gifts. But no, says Paul, all of that is going to pass away when we get to heaven, and we see him. I think 1 John 3:2 is a staggering verse. John says, 'Dear friends, now we're children of God. And what we will be has not yet been fully known, but we know that when Christ appears, we shall be like him, for we shall see him as he is.'

There's a day coming when I'm going to be like Jesus and you will be able to write over my life 'Andy is patient, Andy is kind...' and so on. I'm going to be like Jesus – on that day I'm going to be made perfect. All the chips, all the baggage will be gone, all the rebellion that holds me back will be all gone. I'm going to be like Jesus. I'll be made perfect in love. Wow!

The heartbeat of my relationship with God is not that I found him, but that he found me and rescued me. The key thing is not that I know him, but that he knows me. And a day really is coming when we'll be fully known. In relation to all this, Paul brings this massively challenging word: 'When I was a child, I talked like a child, I thought like a child, I reasoned like a child. When I became a man, I put the ways of childhood behind me' (v11).

Perhaps Paul was thinking about his former days when he thought he was the big Pharisee of Pharisees and he went out rampantly, fervently, with hatred in his heart, to wipe out the church of Jesus. But then he met Jesus on the Damascus road, and he became just as radical, just as fervent but in his love rather than his hatred. It's only Jesus who can do that, isn't it? Only Jesus can transform the human heart. Paul was able to write these beautiful words that he could have never written before seeing Jesus.

So here's the big $64 million question for us, that puts into proper perspective the worth of everything I've done in the last 40 years of being a Christian, or 30 years of trying to build a ministry for him. It's not 'Have I grown in knowledge?' Not, 'Have I become a better leader or developed my God-given gifts in some way?' Not, 'Have I got any letters after my name?' but, 'Have I become mature in *agape* love?' How about you? Allow the Holy Spirit to speak that question into your heart: Have you become mature in love?

Of course, the very best we can offer is like looking in an ancient, blurry metal mirror. You could just about pick your face out, but it was very unclear. That's what it's like now. Even the best efforts of the most sacrificial Christians – even the Mother Teresas or the Jackie Pullingers or the Heidi Bakers of this world – even those we most aspire to be like in their love for Jesus and love for others are just like a blurred mirror compared to the glory to come. Then it'll be 'face to face'. Then we'll be the perfect image of love in Jesus.

Paul wraps it all up with the final verse of the chapter. 'Now these three remain: faith, hope and love. But the greatest of these is love' (v13). It's impossible to know Christ without faith. Faith in Jesus unlocks all these benefits. And hope – our great hope is in heaven for eternity. It's what keeps us going through all the trials and difficulties and challenges of life, our hope of eternity. But there'll be a day when we won't need faith because we'll see him face to face. And there'll be a day when our hope will be fulfilled. But on that day, love will continue. The only thing that will continue is God's perfect love, on into eternity. God, let us grow in your love!

As we close off 1 Corinthians 13, I want to take a little diversion into the last chapter of the Gospel of John because it's a perfect example of the kind of love that Paul is talking about here.

John 21 is a chapter that's just full of drama. It starts with Peter, the rock upon whom Jesus was going to build his church, the miracle man, the great leader, now brought down low. Peter had denied Jesus and brought down curses on his head. Now, on the other side of the cross, Peter was a broken and depressed man. His whole world had fallen apart. And because he was still a leader, he'd led the other disciples back into fishing. At the start of John's Gospel, they laid down their nets and followed Christ. Now all Peter can think to do is pick them back up again.

So we see them all out fishing and once again having a whole night where, just like three years previously, they catch nothing. So Jesus re-enacts the miracle that he did to call them into ministry in the first place – a supernatural haul at completely the wrong time of the day. And then a voice from the shore Peter would know anywhere: 'Fellas, have you caught anything?' It's Jesus. He's risen from the dead. He's conquered sin and death and he's reaching out to a bunch of dirty sinners in the language they can understand. Peter knows who it is, and he jumps into the water and swims as fast as he can towards Jesus on the shore.

The last time Peter saw Jesus, he was standing by a coal fire. A slave girl said to him, 'You know that guy, you've got the same accent. In fact, you're one of his disciples,' and Peter said, 'I don't even know that man... I want nothing to do with him.' He denied Jesus three times and he ran off and wept bitterly. At his friend's time of greatest need, just as Jesus had predicted, and he had said, 'No way I'm going to deny you. Even if all this lot deny you, I'm not going to deny you. Peter, the rock's never going to deny you...' and yet that's exactly what he did.

And now, here's the risen Jesus making him breakfast on the beach, also over a coal fire. How awesome is Jesus? If I was Jesus, to be honest, I'd have been done with Peter by now. One of my friends, one of my key leaders who I'd invested so much in and at my greatest time of need denied me, cursed me, ran off and abandoned me just at the time I needed him most. If it was me, it'd have sounded something like, 'You know, Pete, this is going to take some time, mate. We have to work some serious issues through – and even then you're never going back to the position of key leadership. You're done now.' Thank God I'm not Jesus.

Here's what Jesus actually does: He re-enacts the miracle of the fish, he builds a coal fire... takes him right back to the beginning. And then he gives Peter the chance to make three public declarations and reaffirmations to cancel out his three denials. And he shares with Peter again the task of shepherding the sheep, tending the lambs. He's amazing, isn't he? In his love he says, if you love me, do what I do. If you love me, love these little ones, these vulnerable ones. Bring them into my sheepfold so they can spend all eternity with me and experience my incredible *agape* love.

Give me more of that kind of love! Three times by the coal fire, Jesus says to Peter, 'Simon, son of John.' If you recall, Jesus had renamed him Peter – 'Rocky' or 'the Rock on which I'm going to build my church' – his leadership name. But now he's gone back to 'Simon, son of John'. It must have been a little bit of a dagger. The old guy, back to his old nature.

And the word for love, fascinatingly, changes too. Initially, he says, 'Do you love me?' (John 21:15-16) using the word *agape* or divine love. He's asking, 'Have you got love that never gives up? Love that keeps no record of wrongs? Love that's kind and patient? Have you got that kind of love?' Peter just hangs his head.

So Jesus actually lowers his aim, and says, 'Do you *philio* me?' (v17) – another Greek word for love. A word that means friendship, affection, fondness, but not the sacrificial grace-filled love wrapped up in *agape*. And Simon says. 'Lord, you know all things. You know that I love you.' Then right there, totally undeserved, Jesus recommissions him, to feed his sheep and follow him. Peter the Rock is restored and grows into this incredible leader, moving in the gifts of the Spirit, leading this revival movement because of the *agape* love of Jesus.

Failure is never final with God. No matter how desperate our failure or how deep our shame, he can forgive us. He can renew us and he can restore us and he can use us again. Someone you know may have bitterly let Jesus down. Maybe you yourself have. But failure isn't final because his love never fails. It is never-ending. He's always ready to forgive and restore. It's his heart.

A PRAYER

Lord, I pray that you will let your love grow in us, that we will become more mature in your love, that you give us opportunities today to demonstrate your love. Let us be people filled with Jesus and let us always be willing to forgive.

Help us to reach out to brothers and sisters who are carrying shame and rejection today. There are millions of them in our nation. Bring them back into your fold. Help us Lord, to feed your little lambs and care for your sheep.

Amen.

1 CORINTHIANS 14:1-40

HUNGRY HEARTS

1 CORINTHIANS 14:1–40

Follow the way of love and eagerly desire gifts of the Spirit, especially prophecy. For anyone who speaks in a tongue does not speak to people but to God. Indeed, no one understands them; they utter mysteries by the Spirit. But the one who prophesies speaks to people for their strengthening, encouraging and comfort. Anyone who speaks in a tongue edifies themselves, but the one who prophesies edifies the church. I would like every one of you to speak in tongues, but I would rather have you prophesy. The one who prophesies is greater than the one who speaks in tongues, unless someone interprets, so that the church may be edified.

Now, brothers and sisters, if I come to you and speak in tongues, what good will I be to you, unless I bring you some revelation or knowledge or prophecy or word of instruction? Even in the case of lifeless things that make sounds, such as the pipe or harp, how will anyone know what tune is being played unless there is a distinction in the notes? Again, if the trumpet does not sound a clear call, who will get ready for battle? So it is with you. Unless you speak intelligible words with your tongue, how will anyone know what you are saying? You will just be speaking into the air. Undoubtedly there are all sorts of languages in the world, yet none of them is without meaning. If then I do not grasp the meaning of what someone is saying, I am a foreigner to the speaker, and the speaker is a foreigner to me. So it is with you. Since you are eager for gifts of the Spirit, try to excel in those that build up the church.

For this reason the one who speaks in a tongue should pray that they may interpret what they say. For if I pray in a tongue, my spirit prays, but my mind is unfruitful. So what shall I do? I will pray with my spirit, but I will also pray with my understanding; I will sing with my spirit, but I will also sing with my understanding. Otherwise when you are praising God in the Spirit, how can someone else, who is now put in the position of an inquirer, say "Amen" to your thanksgiving, since they do not know what you are saying? You are giving thanks well enough, but no one else is edified.

I thank God that I speak in tongues more than all of you. But in the church I would rather speak five intelligible words to instruct others than ten thousand words in a tongue.

Brothers and sisters, stop thinking like children. In regard to evil be infants, but in your thinking be adults. In the Law it is written:

"With other tongues and through the lips of foreigners I will speak to this people, but even then they will not listen to me, says the Lord."

Tongues, then, are a sign, not for believers but for unbelievers; prophecy, however, is not for unbelievers but for believers. So if the whole church comes together and everyone speaks in tongues, and inquirers or unbelievers come in, will they not say that you are out of your mind? But if an unbeliever or an inquirer comes in while everyone is prophesying, they are convicted of sin and are brought under judgment by all, as the secrets of their hearts are laid bare. So they will fall down and worship God, exclaiming, "God is really among you!"

What then shall we say, brothers and sisters? When you come together, each of you has a hymn, or a word of instruction, a revelation, a tongue or an interpretation. Everything must be done so that the church may be built up. If anyone speaks in a tongue, two – or at the most three – should speak, one at a time, and someone must interpret. If there is no interpreter, the speaker should keep quiet in the church and speak to himself and to God.

Two or three prophets should speak, and the others should weigh carefully what is said. And if a revelation comes to someone who is sitting down, the first speaker should stop. For you can all prophesy in turn so that everyone may be instructed and encouraged. The spirits of prophets are subject to the control of prophets. For God is not a God of disorder but of peace – as in all the congregations of the Lord's people.

Women should remain silent in the churches. They are not allowed to speak, but must be in submission, as the law says. If they want to inquire about something, they should ask their own husbands at home; for it is disgraceful for a woman to speak in the church.

Or did the word of God originate with you? Or are you the only people it has reached? If anyone thinks they are a prophet or otherwise gifted by the Spirit, let them acknowledge that what I am writing to you is the Lord's command. But if anyone ignores this, they will themselves be ignored.

Therefore, my brothers and sisters, be eager to prophesy, and do not forbid speaking in tongues. But everything should be done in a fitting and orderly way.

Two beautiful things were happening in the Corinthian church as they grew. They are the same two things that I long to happen in Manchester and wherever The Message is at work.

The first thing is that all sorts of broken people were coming to Christ. Corinth was a sex-satiated city and as real people came to Christ, you can imagine the implications for the church of all these people with a desperate lack of love and a desperate need for attention. Even if they weren't prostitutes, they were 'party people' and they surely brought that culture into the church. They were people with hungry hearts and it would have shown up in their worship as people brought their brokenness to church and bit by bit God worked through that.

The second thing is that the Spirit was being poured out in unprecedented measure. The fulfilment of Joel's prophecy was happening right there in Corinth, where Peter brought that word right at the birth of the church – 'In the last days, God says, I will pour out my Spirit on all people. Your sons and daughters will prophesy, your young men will see visions, your old men will dream dreams' (Acts 2:17, Joel 2:28).

Whenever broken people gather in the church – and we're all broken to some degree – there's always a mix of the flesh and the Spirit. Paul's strong desire is that everything is done in a 'fitting and orderly way.' That's because in Corinth, it was anything but – it was chaotic. Outsiders were coming in and were confused. What is this all about? These are crazy people!

How many people feel alienated by church today? How many people are turned off by the weird language and the weird clothes? And it's not just the conservatives or the traditional churches, charismatic churches can be just as weird to outsiders. We always have to have one eye on those who don't know Jesus. In the Corinthian church too, all kinds of strange things were going on, so Paul lays down some foundational principles.

It can be summed up in his first words: 'Follow the way of love and eagerly desire gifts of the Spirit.' That's a beautiful balance. It's always love first. Without love, we should just pack up and go home. We should shut the doors if we're not a people of love who pour out love to each other and to a world in need. It's the unique priority and foundation of everything. Get that right, and then eagerly desire the spiritual gifts. Our God responds to passion – it touches his heart. He's looking for a passionate people. So how passionate are we for the gifts of the Spirit? When the Bible says, we should 'eagerly desire' the gifts of the Spirit, we should be passionate for them to be manifested in our lives.

My prayer is always for the gift of the evangelist. I long for a group of people in every nation on earth that are passionate for the gift of the evangelist – soul winners in Jesus' name, cool, real Bible-loving, Spirit-filled evangelists who bring in a harvest. You might say, 'But hang on a minute! Paul doesn't say "especially evangelism" – he says, "especially prophecy!"' But you know what I want? Prophetic evangelists. Let me explain what I mean.

The gift of prophecy is not as we sometimes imagine it – foretelling the future. God can use it like that but more often prophecy is telling people things that can only be known by divine revelation – and that's through the scriptures primarily. That's why what we need is evangelists with a good understanding of the Bible and who can speak it out in a language that people can understand.

Evangelists, wake up! We have to be prophetic, speaking out God's word to our culture. God, give us those kind of evangelists! Give us those kind of preachers. I want our Bible teachers to not bring a few platitudes, just to tell young people how special they are, but to teach the Bible in the power of the Spirit, prophetically.

Even when we've done all that, we still absolutely rely on the rain from heaven. We can bring the word of the Lord, but we're still relying on God to do his bit – to bring that miraculous divine revelation so people who have scales over their eyes have them suddenly opened. Don't you want verse 25 to happen where you live? I do! In schools and prisons and tough communities where Paul says if we can get this right, 'the secrets of people's hearts will be laid bare... they'll fall down and worship God, and exclaim, "God is really among you."' It happens when people hear the word of the

Lord, understand the word of the Lord, bring it prophetically, and God brings his revelation. Do it, Lord!

Paul though, knew very well that that wasn't always the case where he was. He knew there were people flaunting and abusing the gift of prophecy. There still are. Sadly, I've seen the gift of prophecy misused and abused over the years. Quite often prophetic words can be used to make people look good or feel better, or even manipulate them. It can be very upsetting and harmful. It's so wrong, so scary. That's why in 1 Thessalonians 5:20-21 he brings this corrective classic pragmatic approach to prophecy. Paul says. 'Don't treat prophecy with contempt. Test everything, hold onto the good.' I love that. Don't, whatever you do, treat prophecy with contempt. I don't believe people should say, 'Thus saith the Lord.' I think people should say, 'I think this is what the Lord might be saying... I might be wrong, but I've been praying and I think this may be what the Lord is saying.' There's a humility about that in my mind, and if it is the word of the Lord, it's going to hit home just as hard.

I've also seen prophecy used very well. Used properly, prophecy will always build up and edify. Recently I was in our prayer room. Isaac Sali, who is an amazing man of God with a track record of prophecy, started prophesying a word of encouragement over me of all the Lord is going to fulfil in this next season. He said the Lord was going to do double because he had provided. Later this word was confirmed by our Germany team leader who had been watching the prayer session via a remote video link, and got in touch and said whilst he was prophesying, I was on double screen for three minutes. It stepped up my faith and expectation in an extraordinary way.

It built me up. It edified me. The key thing is that building up and edifying – it says it no less than seven times in this passage, Paul says prophecy is meant to edify. Church should be an edifying, illuminating experience where we receive that divine revelation. That's why when we gather as Christians we should be on tiptoes of excitement. We should go expectant that God could reveal something to us that will utterly change our situations, change our expectations and, as a result, change our lives.

Which brings us to the gift of tongues, which Paul mentions repeatedly here. Tongues, too, are meant to edify the body. Which is why Paul has a beef with everybody babbling on in tongues at the same time. Who's edified by that? Paul says when we're together we're meant to build up the body. The whole thing isn't meant to be looking vertically, but also looking horizontally. I need to continually ask: how is what I do in church encouraging my brothers and sisters? Paul says, whenever someone brings a tongue in the church they should have an interpretation. I mean, we largely ignore that in the church. Occasionally we hear interpretations when somebody speaks in tongues, but not often.

Funny isn't it, how we pick and choose bits of the Bible and that we accept and practise. But it seems like quite a strong word from Paul. Otherwise tongues should be just for personal edification. Paul doesn't diss the gift of tongues, far from it – he says, 'I speak more in tongues than any anyone else.' He uses the gift, but he uses it primarily for personal edification, for his walk with the Lord.

....

A PRAYER

Give us a hungry heart, God.

Give us a heart for you and your gifts and for the ability
to use them well. May they always be offered on the
foundation of love, always to build up the body. Give us
a desire for serving others with the gifts you give us.

Amen.

....

1 CORINTHIANS 15:1-34

THE RESURRECTION....
PAST, PRESENT AND FUTURE POWER

1 CORINTHIANS 15:1-34

Now, brothers and sisters, I want to remind you of the gospel I preached to you, which you received and on which you have taken your stand. By this gospel you are saved, if you hold firmly to the word I preached to you. Otherwise, you have believed in vain.

For what I received I passed on to you as of first importance: that Christ died for our sins according to the Scriptures, that he was buried, that he was raised on the third day according to the Scriptures, and that he appeared to Cephas, and then to the Twelve. After that, he appeared to more than five hundred of the brothers and sisters at the same time, most of whom are still living, though some have fallen asleep. Then he appeared to James, then to all the apostles, and last of all he appeared to me also, as to one abnormally born.

For I am the least of the apostles and do not even deserve to be called an apostle, because I persecuted the church of God. But by the grace of God I am what I am, and his grace to me was not without effect. No, I worked harder than all of them – yet not I, but the grace of God that was with me. Whether, then, it is I or they, this is what we preach, and this is what you believed.

But if it is preached that Christ has been raised from the dead, how can some of you say that there is no resurrection of the dead? If there is no resurrection of the dead, then not even Christ has been raised. And if Christ has not been raised, our preaching is useless and so is your faith. More than that, we are then found to be false witnesses about God, for we have testified about God that he raised Christ from the dead. But he did not raise him if in fact the dead are not raised. For if the dead are not raised, then Christ has not been raised either. And if Christ has not been raised, your faith is futile; you are still in your sins. Then those also who have fallen asleep in Christ are lost. If only for this life we have hope in Christ, we are of all people most to be pitied.

But Christ has indeed been raised from the dead, the firstfruits of those who have fallen asleep. For since death came through a man, the resurrection of the dead comes also through a man. For as in Adam all die, so in Christ all will be made alive. But each in turn: Christ, the firstfruits; then, when he comes, those who belong to him. Then the end will come, when he hands over the kingdom to God the Father after he has destroyed all dominion, authority and power. For he must reign until he has put all his enemies under his feet. The last enemy to be destroyed is death. For he "has put everything under his feet." Now when it says that "everything" has been put under him, it is clear that this does not include God himself, who put everything under Christ. When he has done this, then the Son himself will be made subject to him who put everything under him, so that God may be all in all.

Now if there is no resurrection, what will those do who are baptised for the dead? If the dead are not raised at all, why are people baptised for them? And as for us, why do we endanger ourselves every hour? I face death every day – yes, just as surely as I boast about you in Christ Jesus our Lord. If I fought wild beasts in Ephesus with no more than human hopes, what have I gained? If the dead are not raised,

"Let us eat and drink, for tomorrow we die."

Do not be misled: "Bad company corrupts good character." Come back to your senses as you ought, and stop sinning; for there are some who are ignorant of God – I say this to your shame.

....

The Corinthian church was like Paul's problem child. He'd surely left Corinth with a huge sense of encouragement that God had moved in this materialistic, wild-living, pagan city. He'd planted a church and it had taken root. He went off on his missionary journeys full of faith and excitement.

But then he started to get the letters… about crazy goings-on in the church with these new believers. They were gathering for worship, having communion where some would get drunk while some would be left hungry. They were forgetting the poor. They were falling out with each other, and not just petty divisions, but lawsuits amongst believers. There was weirdness going on with spiritual gifts in their services.

Paul knew the main reason for all this stuff was that they hadn't really understood the gospel. They'd heard Paul preach the gospel, and maybe they'd made a commitment to Christ. But they hadn't understood it in the way they needed to.

Sound teaching, if it's really accepted and believed, always results in godly lifestyle. If you're all over the place as a Christian – up and down like a yo-yo, giving in to temptation all the time, it means you don't really understand the amazing truth of the gospel. It's not taken root in your life.

That's why Paul starts 1 Corinthians 15 by saying, 'Now, brothers and sisters, I want to remind you of the gospel I preached to you… that Christ died for our sins according to the Scriptures, that he was buried, that he was raised on the third day according to the Scriptures.'

I love that Paul gets straight to the resurrection. He says, look, Jesus rose from the dead – just go and have a chat with some of the people who met him! There were 500 in one meeting and lots of them would have still been alive. The way to prove that Jesus rose from the dead is that loads of people actually met him! And we can say the same – the way to prove Jesus is risen from the dead is that around two billion people or so on Planet Earth will tell you that they have met him.

So the question is this: if you believe what Paul says in this passage – that Jesus is Lord, that he died for our sins, that he rose again, and as a result we have eternal life... what are you doing with your life? Corinthians, what are you doing with your life? Mancunians, what are you doing with your life? Wherever you're reading this, what are you doing with your life? If you really believe that Jesus is Lord of all eternity, that he left heaven and came to earth, that he lived this remarkable life, that he died a criminal's death on a cross, that he rose again from the dead, that he conquered sin and death... what are you doing with your life?

It seems that in Corinth people were losing faith in these basic truths. And that meant they were losing their power and were losing their authority. Same today, right? Look at a denomination that's lost its power and authority.... It's because they've moved away from the gospel. Look at a Christian charity that's doing good works but no longer the world-changing movement they're meant to be.... It's because they've moved away from the simplicity of the gospel of the Lord Jesus. They may still say they believe it, but they no longer behave like it.

The way to change the world is to have the gospel absolutely front and centre, like a lamp on a stand. That's the only message we've got that can change the world. This is what I tell our staff: never forget if you work for this organisation, or volunteer or are involved anywhere around the world, remember we're called The Message. If you want a charity that does good, cares for the poor, tries to lobby government and change policies, but isn't concerned that the gospel is front and centre, other charities are available. This one is always going to have the message of the cross and the resurrection front and centre. And you know what I've learned? The more we keep that gospel of Jesus Christ front and centre, the more God blesses us.

We recently did a brilliant event called 'Transformed lives, transforming communities'. In many of the communities in which we work, there's terrible domestic violence and self-harm, addiction, crime and all kinds of brokenness. The only way those communities are going to be transformed is more transformed lives – people whose hearts have been transformed by the gospel.

On the night we heard some of the incredible stories that have come out of our Community Groceries and Eden teams – beautiful stories of women receiving Christ, speaking of their joy in him and their relationship with him. We also heard from Paul, one of our Eden team leaders, who came to Christ out of a chaotic lifestyle and then led loads of his mates to the Lord. They've all since joined the Eden team! That's how you transform communities – by the power of the gospel changing human hearts. That's how the poor will be uplifted, family life will be blessed, society will be changed, the prisons will be emptied – when the gospel is lifted high.

Our nation may be richer than ever, but in many ways we're poorer than ever – worse mental health, more suicide, more marriage breakdown, the prisons are full. Can't we see we need the gospel preached to our nation like never before? We need it to take root in human hearts like never before! That means we need people who will 'take a stand', as Paul says – who are prepared to take a stand on this gospel, to stake their future, their reputation, even their lives on it.

One man who did that was a guy called CT Studd. He was a man who had everything in worldly terms. He was from a fabulously wealthy family. He went to Eton, the best school in the world. He went to Cambridge University, probably the best university in the world. He was a brilliant sportsman. He became England's cricket captain. He committed his life to Christ, but he wasn't really on fire until his brother got seriously ill and looked like he was going to die. CT Studd wrote in his journal, 'What is all this fame and flattery worth when a man comes face to face with eternity?'

So he gave up all his vast inheritance. He gave it all away to various mission agencies. He turned away from the cricket that he loved so much and went to the mission field. He went to China, to India and then to Africa against medical advice. The drive for missions kept him going until he died in the Congo in 1931. By this time, he'd formed WEC, which stands for the World Evangelisation Crusade. Today, WEC have over 1,800 missionaries in many of the poorest nations with the gospel front and centre.

CT Studd was famous for saying, 'Only one life, 'twill soon be passed. Only what's done for Jesus will last.' His most famous saying is, 'If Jesus Christ be God and died for me there, no sacrifice can be too great for me to make for him.'

I long for young men and women to join The Message who think like this. People who say, 'I've only got one life – why would I not want to focus on lifting up the gospel? What I would not put my energies and my talents – whether it's rapping or singing or dancing – as a platform for that gospel?' For others, it's making sure behind the scenes it's run with excellence. Bringing our very, very best so Jesus can be known and so this gospel can be heard.

Eternity is going to be so long. This is my one shot – it will soon be over. If Jesus Christ is God and died for me, then no sacrifice can be too great. Why wouldn't I be like CT Studd, and follow Jesus to the end of the world, or the end of my street, with his gospel on my lips?

Everybody deserves to hear this gospel in language they can understand because it's the power of God for salvation of anyone who believes. We have to take personal responsibility. Sometimes we can think it's someone else's job – it's the preacher's job, it's the evangelist's job. No, it's our job – we've been commissioned. We've been charged to share this good news. It's your job. It's my job. Who else is going to tell the world? The secular humanists aren't going to tell them about the cross and the resurrection and the soon return of Jesus, are they? We've got to tell them – it needs to be on our lips and in our lives. We need to be obsessed with this glorious gospel. Let's give it everything!

....

A PRAYER

Jesus, I pray for a people rising up all over the world with your gospel on their lips and in their lives. People who stand firm on this gospel while others are falling left and right. We're firm on the solid rock that Jesus is Lord. He came to earth. He left heaven and came to earth. He died on the cross and he's alive today and I pray as a result many, many, many will receive the resurrection power of the gospel in their own lives.

We pray God that we'll see a move of your Spirit, a salvation movement of transformed lives transforming communities. Thank you, God, that we get to be part of that. And not just here in Manchester, but all over the world.

Amen.

....

1 CORINTHIANS 15:35-58

THE ME I WAS MEANT TO BE

But someone will ask, "How are the dead raised? With what kind of body will they come?" How foolish! What you sow does not come to life unless it dies. When you sow, you do not plant the body that will be, but just a seed, perhaps of wheat or of something else. But God gives it a body as he has determined, and to each kind of seed he gives its own body. Not all flesh is the same: People have one kind of flesh, animals have another, birds another and fish another. There are also heavenly bodies and there are earthly bodies; but the splendour of the heavenly bodies is one kind, and the splendour of the earthly bodies is another. The sun has one kind of splendour, the moon another and the stars another; and star differs from star in splendour.

So will it be with the resurrection of the dead. The body that is sown is perishable, it is raised imperishable; it is sown in dishonour, it is raised in glory; it is sown in weakness, it is raised in power; it is sown a natural body, it is raised a spiritual body.

If there is a natural body, there is also a spiritual body. So it is written: "The first man Adam became a living being"; the last Adam, a life-giving spirit. The spiritual did not come first, but the natural, and after that the spiritual. The first man was of the dust of the earth; the second man is of heaven. As was the earthly man, so are those who are of the earth; and as is the heavenly man, so also are those who are of heaven. And just as we have borne the image of the earthly man, so shall we bear the image of the heavenly man.

I declare to you, brothers and sisters, that flesh and blood cannot inherit the kingdom of God, nor does the perishable inherit the imperishable. Listen, I tell you a mystery: We will not all sleep, but we will all be changed – in a flash, in the twinkling of an eye, at the last trumpet. For the trumpet will sound, the dead will be raised imperishable, and we will be changed. For the perishable must clothe itself with the imperishable, and the mortal with immortality. When the perishable has been clothed with the imperishable, and the mortal with immortality, then the saying that is written will come true: "Death has been swallowed up in victory."

"Where, O death, is your victory?
  Where, O death, is your sting?"

The sting of death is sin, and the power of sin is the law. But thanks be to God! He gives us the victory through our Lord Jesus Christ.

Therefore, my dear brothers and sisters, stand firm. Let nothing move you. Always give yourselves fully to the work of the Lord, because you know that your labour in the Lord is not in vain.

....

Paul was an incredible strategist. He went from key city to key city planting churches. He seemed to have it all mapped out in his mind under the inspiration of the Holy Spirit. He was an amazing leader, an incredible pioneer. He had huge faith. He had a great mind – just read the theology that he was able to explain in simple language. But you know what perhaps Paul's greatest asset of all was? He had a heavenly perspective.

In one sense, Paul was done with this world when, as an angry terrorist, determined to wipe out the church of Jesus, he had an encounter with Jesus, the risen Jesus, on the road to Damascus in Acts 9. He said a light from heaven flashed all around him and that light never left him. From the moment he met Jesus on the road he knew that 'for me to live is Christ, and to die is gain' (Phil 1:21). He was granted a vision of heaven that never left him. Some people say you can be so heavenly minded that you're no earthly good. I disagree. Paul had such a heavenly perspective he was loads of earthly good!

I heard about a little girl who crawled up onto her grandfather's knee, and she said, 'Granddad, make a noise like a frog.' So he went, 'Ribbit, ribbit, ribbit!'

The little girl ran off to her mother and said, 'Mum, great news! We're going to Disney World!' And the mother says, 'Why are you saying we're going to Disney World? I didn't say we were going to Disney World.'

'Yes, you did,' the girl replied. 'You said when Granddad croaks we can go to Disney World!'

That's a bad joke, but it reminds us of the truth that we're all going to croak. When you're young and fit and healthy, maybe you don't think about it much, but the more life moves on, you start to realise you're going to die one day. This life is so short, and Paul wants the Corinthian church to wake up. To stop getting so wrapped up in earthly stuff – like petty divisions or flaunting their gifts or forgetting the poor.

A vision of heaven stops all that. Let's fix our eyes on Jesus. Let's fix our eyes on where we're going. Let's have our hearts set determinedly on heaven. Let's map out our course – not just for a few years on this planet, but the eternal course of our life where we're going – a place too glorious for words. A future that literally beggars belief beyond description.

Paul is saying, 'Come on Corinthians – wake up to where you're going to be for all eternity. Get your eyes off yourselves and this present age that's so me-centred and materialistic and fix your eyes on eternity – it'll change everything.'

Now, I don't think I've got a big issue with self-esteem, but the lockdowns were not good for the way I think about myself. I spent far too long staring at myself on Zoom, looking at every wrinkle and flaw. I realise that my body is gradually wasting away and as I get older, I'm asking, do I really want this body for eternity? Well, no, I don't. And the good news is I'm not going to have it. When I'm resurrected and transformed, according to the Bible, I'll be transformed to be like Jesus. This passage tells us about my new body that's to come and the good news is I'll have an amazing body that's able to contain the full glory of God.

There's two things the Bible tells me about that body. The first thing is, there's total transformation. It's a new body for a new heaven and a new earth. I'm going to be part of that transformation. And the second thing the Bible tells me is there's clear continuity. It will be me, but it'll be like the difference between a seed and a beautiful flower that's grown into everything it's meant to be. You'll recognise me, but I'll be transformed into the me I was meant to be.

Are you looking forward to that day when you're free of all the chips and baggage that hold you back right now? The stain of sin and disease? Are you looking forward to being wonderfully, beautifully free, free from tiredness and weakness and death? Free from it all, free in Jesus? Well, that's my future, and it's yours, if you are a Jesus follower. Hebrews 7:16 calls it 'the indestructible life', and the Lord wants Christians to set our hearts on it – that we, like Paul, are so heavenly minded that we're loads of earthly use.

I love Joni Eareckson Tada. I remember reading her book as a new Christian decades ago and been so inspired by this beautiful, talented young woman who had a diving accident and tragically ended up in a wheelchair. She prayed for healing which never came and yet she has been a role model of gutsy Christianity over decades. She said this: 'My suffering and training is a lifelong process. And it will be until I go to be with Christ in heaven.'

She's got a heavenly perspective. Maybe she'd love to be healed, but she's prepared to wait for a while now and use whatever is thrown at her. It sounds a bit like Paul to me after his terrible suffering and training that he describes in 2 Corinthians. He suffered some of the worst things that could be thrown at a person, yet he describes them as 'light and momentary troubles that are earning for me an eternal glory that far outweighs them all' (4:17).

That's a totally correct perspective. What could touch a man or a woman like that? When this transformation, this metamorphosis takes place, in 'the twinkling of an eye' (v52). The blinking of the eye takes about a 30th of a second – the twinkling of an eye is hundreds of times faster than that. That's how quick I'll go from this body to that body. In a flash, all the pain of sin and all the discouragement and all the hard work of being in the flesh will be gone.

My mum is 89 years old now and because of her faith in Christ, death has really lost its sting for her. When we pray together, there's a sense that she's so ready for heaven. Of course, she wants to see her great-grandkids and all that, but actually, she's just good to go – she's so looking forward to heaven. I believe for Christians like my mum it's going to be a little jump into eternity, a little step. It will be amazing and glorious – there'll be none of the arthritis and none of the things that hold her back anymore.

Paul calls it 'a mystery' (v51) and I think it should make us feel gutted when we read that. Similarly, when he says the gospel's a mystery to so many in 1 Corinthians 4:1 and in Colossians 1:26-27.

How sad that so many people are living with their eggs in the wrong basket. Living with all their efforts and all their energies set on this one short life. It's wrong. We know stuff that the world doesn't know and it's wrong that the good news of eternal life is a mystery to so many – people on our street, even our friends and family.

They need to know there's a glorious future for them because of what Christ did on the cross. He died and then he rose again, and because he rose, we're going to rise if we make him Lord and repent of our sins.

There's a charge here to us to wake up to our bright, great, amazing, eternal future – to wake up to heaven where there'll be no addiction, no self-harming, no jealousies and egos, just beautiful freedom in Christ. And so he says 'Thanks be to God who gives us the victory in our Lord Jesus Christ. Therefore, my dear brothers and sisters, stand firm. Let nothing move you. Always give yourself fully to the work of the Lord, because you know that your labour is not in vain' (verses 57-58).

Three things, then, to wrap up this chapter and Paul's amazing vision of eternity....

First, 'Stand firm. Let nothing move you.' Let's let nothing move us from proclaiming the good news of eternal life. Don't let temptations and trinkets distract you. Let nothing move you from this gospel. Wake up to the power of it. I'm going to live forever. I don't deserve it, but my future is bright.

Second, 'Always give yourself fully to the work of the Lord.' You know what the work of the Lord is – it's loving people and serving people and developing a prayer walk with Jesus and relationship with him and then sharing that good news with others, pouring out your life on that. Always give yourself fully to that work.

Finally, 'You know that your labour is not in vain.' Only what's done for Jesus will last – but listen, what's done for Jesus *will* last. Know for sure, you'll never regret a penny you gave to the work of the Lord. You'll never regret a single prayer, or act of service. You'll never regret a time you opened your mouth and told people the way to eternal life. Those things will last forever.

....

A PRAYER

Lord, let heaven come to earth more and more in
our own lives. We know that only what's done for
you will last and we want our lives to last, not just
for a few years here on earth, but on into eternity.

Thank you for the new body able to contain your glory.
Help us to look forward to that and say for now 'for
me to live is Christ.' Fill us, Lord, and spur us on.

Amen.

....

1 CORINTHIANS 16:1-24

THE CHURCH THAT SPREADS RAPIDLY AND GROWS IN POWER

Now about the collection for the Lord's people: Do what I told the Galatian churches to do. On the first day of every week, each one of you should set aside a sum of money in keeping with your income, saving it up, so that when I come no collections will have to be made. Then, when I arrive, I will give letters of introduction to the men you approve and send them with your gift to Jerusalem. If it seems advisable for me to go also, they will accompany me.

After I go through Macedonia, I will come to you – for I will be going through Macedonia. Perhaps I will stay with you for a while, or even spend the winter, so that you can help me on my journey, wherever I go. For I do not want to see you now and make only a passing visit; I hope to spend some time with you, if the Lord permits. But I will stay on at Ephesus until Pentecost, because a great door for effective work has opened to me, and there are many who oppose me.

When Timothy comes, see to it that he has nothing to fear while he is with you, for he is carrying on the work of the Lord, just as I am. No one, then, should treat him with contempt. Send him on his way in peace so that he may return to me. I am expecting him along with the brothers.

Now about our brother Apollos: I strongly urged him to go to you with the brothers. He was quite unwilling to go now, but he will go when he has the opportunity.

Be on your guard; stand firm in the faith; be courageous; be strong. Do everything in love.

You know that the household of Stephanas were the first converts in Achaia, and they have devoted themselves to the service of the Lord's people. I urge you, brothers and sisters, to submit to such people and to everyone who joins in the work and labors at it. I was glad when

Stephanas, Fortunatus and Achaicus arrived, because they have supplied what was lacking from you. For they refreshed my spirit and yours also. Such men deserve recognition.

The churches in the province of Asia send you greetings. Aquila and Priscilla greet you warmly in the Lord, and so does the church that meets at their house. All the brothers and sisters here send you greetings. Greet one another with a holy kiss.

I, Paul, write this greeting in my own hand.

If anyone does not love the Lord, let that person be cursed! Come, Lord!

The grace of the Lord Jesus be with you.

My love to all of you in Christ Jesus. Amen.

....

In this final chapter, Paul's excitement about the potential of the church in Corinth starts to grow, despite all its problems. Paul was a man who was able to mine reserves of Holy Spirit joy in the most remarkable way. Despite all the challenges and all the suffering he faced, Paul's letter bubbles over with joy. He seems to have learned to live with the tension that maybe life isn't what it's meant to be, maybe ministry isn't going great in certain areas. Yet joy still carries us forward. Paul's heart, as he brings this letter in to land, is overflowing with joy because he sees a church that really could be amazing if they can just get their act together.

He sees a church that he describes in this letter as interdependent. Not independent, interdependent. Paul is passionate that this church in Corinth supports the mother church in Jerusalem. He tells them to take up an offering, not for themselves, but to bless their brothers and sisters in Jerusalem, who are suffering. There was a severe famine going on in Jerusalem and all kind of persecution going on directed towards that baby church.

There's only one church. Not the church in Corinth or the church in Jerusalem. If we could wake up to that, it would be game-changing. I'm so excited by what's happening here in Manchester because it feels like the body of Christ is coming together now in a way that I've never experienced in my lifetime.

How tragic it is that there are around 40,000 different Christian denominations and streams? I believe that's been Satan's great attack on the church since the time of Jesus, since he prayed that we'd be one. Satan has been trying to divide us and split us up to dissipate our effectiveness. If we could just learn to honour and bless and serve and work together despite our differences, it'd be massive for the work of God in this or any other region.

So he speaks about an interdependent church. But he also speaks about a persecuted church. One of the most amazing verses in the New Testament, I think, is this: 'I will stay on at Ephesus until Pentecost, because a great door for effective work has opened to me, and there are many who oppose me.' (v9)

He says, 'I can't come to you right now, much as I want to come personally and deal with all the difficulties and the challenges of this baby church. I can't leave Ephesus right now because I'm in the middle of revival!' The work is growing rapidly, the word of God is spreading, 'a great door of effective work has opened to me' and... 'There are many who oppose me.' That's Paul saying, 'We must be on to something!'

We would imagine, wouldn't we, that effective witness would mean there would be many who are with us – many who are cheering us on, many who are praying, many who are donating, many who are supporting, many who are telling us what a fantastic job we're doing. And yes, that does sometimes go with the territory.

But let's be clear – there are many who are going to oppose us. There are many who are going to oppose us if we teach biblical values about marriage and human sexuality. If we teach that Jesus is the way the truth and the life, the unique son of God, and the only way to Christ. If we teach the cross and the resurrection in all its power, even with humility and even with grace, there will be many who oppose us. Don't be surprised by that.

I've often said I want to experience what the Salvation Army experienced in the late 19th century, where the Spirit of God fell on the poor in unprecedented measure and people were running to the front of Booth's meetings, weeping and flat out in the Holy Spirit. The poorest, most broken members of society, the addicts and the homeless, were flooding into the kingdom. Crime stopped in whole cities under the work of the Salvation Army, and I believe, there's a kind of mandate on The Message Trust to reinvent those days. There are many similarities between how God used them and how he's using us: a focus on the poor, creative mission, music ministry, prison ministry, jobs for ex-offenders, feeding the poor.... Lots of the things we've stumbled on, the Salvation Army did first, and at another level.

What were the five hallmarks of the Salvation Army? Here's what it says in a book I've been reading by Winkie Pratney (what a great name).

The first one was that saving souls was their priority. They were a Salvation Army. They never lost sight of that. The second one was that they were faith-filled. They were willing to risk everything to preach for the lost, the last and the least. The third one was that they loved the poor. They cared for the poor, they had God's heart for the poor and the broken and the marginalised. The fourth one was that they were committed to holy living. The fifth one was that they knew what it was to suffer. They embraced suffering. They were rejected and persecuted and hated here in England.

'From the time William Booth preached his first sermon in Nottingham he was jeered at, mocked and ridiculed. As a woman in Victorian England, Catherine Booth felt the sting of exclusion from society. Throughout the early years of the Army's ministry, its young soldiers had to dodge missiles of rotten fruit, dead animals, rocks and briquettes and crowds. There was a whole movement called the Skeleton Army that set up deliberately in opposition to wreck their meetings and destroy their ministry. Salvationists were roped, punched, kicked, spat on, and pelted with rocks and burning sulphur. Entire gangs of hundreds, even up to thousands, rallied to stop the little holy band but the army marched into town anyway, covered in slime often, but not ashamed, kneeling in the centre of the town, they lifted their battle cry, "Lord Jesus in your name. We claim this city for God" and then they got up to take it, regardless of the opposition.'

Paul knew it. William and Catherine knew it. We don't desire it or look for it, but we shouldn't be surprised when it goes with the territory.

Of course there's encouragement, too. What a great verse this is: 'You know that the household of Stephanas were the first converts in Achaia, and they have devoted themselves to the service of the Lord's people' (v15).

How amazing it is when you see people come to Christ like that. You're not trying to follow them up with a discipleship programme – on the contrary, you can't keep up with them! It's amazing when people hit the ground running like Stephanas' family, his whole household 'devoted themselves.' They'd got stuck in, loving Jesus by serving faithfully. They were a genuinely great family because they'd learned that 'whoever wants to be great amongst you must be your servant' (Matt 20:26). Yes, there were problems and trials and dodgy goings-on in Corinth. But praise God, there were always people like Stephanas to keep you going.

And again, how about verse 19? 'The churches in the province of Asia send you greetings. Aquila and Priscilla greet you warmly in the Lord, and so does the church that meets at their house. All the brothers and sisters here send you greetings…'.

Thank God for beautiful people serving the Lord, who came to Christ and then got on with his mission. Don't you want to be part of that kind of church? Let it be, Lord!

Paul was going through so much – so much pressure, all that persecution, all that imprisonment, all the frustration of Christians being weird in the new churches. He couldn't do it on his own. He needed brothers and sisters to come alongside him and run with him. And as the work grows here at The Message, or whatever church or ministry you're involved with, you and I need those people.

So he wraps up the whole letter by taking the quill in his own hand and almost certainly writes in large letters like he did at the end of Galatians. He wants to leave them with two things: 'The grace of the Lord Jesus be with you' (v23), and 'My love to all of you in Christ Jesus' (v24).

He wants them to know that, despite the rebukes and challenges through the last 16 chapters, he loves them. He loves the greedy, the proud, the drunkards, the selfish, the doctrinally unsound. He loves them. And Jesus loves them, too.

You know, for us in the West 2,000 years later, it's the same old boring stuff. Divisions and conflicts, strange doctrines, strange practices in worship meetings that put people off, leaders on power trips, wrong attitudes and beliefs, and fuzziness about the cross and the resurrection. It's all here in church. All that mess is here.

That's why this letter is so relevant. These things needed tackling, and needed tackling head on. We can't back off from it. We can't just brush it under the carpet because we love people and we're full of grace. No, it needs tackling. But it must be tackled with grace and love. We'll get nowhere without grace and love – we'll just fall out and tragically we'll have one more denomination to add to the list, carving up the body of Christ.

So let's be grace people, grace over everything. People who are committed to the truth, committed to living holy lives, but working it out in great love and compassion for others, as Paul did. As far as it's down to us, let's be unwavering in owning and living out our responsibility to share the good news in words and actions. But let's always do it with a gracious twinkle in our eye. Grace is God's undeserved, unmerited love poured out on others because it's been poured out on us.

That sounds good, doesn't it? Isn't that the kind of church you want to be part of? It's a church that will grow rapidly. And the Word of God will spread throughout the world. And ordinary insignificant people like me and you can be part of that and it's literally the greatest adventure on earth. Why would you want to bother with anything else?

....

A PRAYER

We pray, Lord, that your church will come together like never before in this region and all over the world – one body working together. We pray, Lord, you'll help us when persecution and opposition comes, as things hot up, to be strong in you and to cheer one another on.

Fill us with your Spirit, Lord, so we can do that. We know there's no way on our own we can. But with you, Lord, anything is possible. All for you, Jesus.

Amen.

....

THE MESSAGE TRUST

A burning heart has driven The Message Trust from day one – a heart desperate for people to hear the good news of Jesus and see lives transformed by him.

What started as a bunch of friends going into schools has grown over the past three decades into a global movement which unashamedly shares the gospel with the hardest-to-reach people and communities. So, in schools, on stages, on streets, in prisons and in communities you'll find us sharing the love of Jesus in word and action.

IN SCHOOLS...

Telling young people about Jesus is at the core of our DNA. If you want to see society and families changed for good, start by telling the next generation. So, across the UK, Germany, Canada and South Africa, you'll finding our cutting-edge creative mission teams in schools, churches, communities and at events telling young people about their true value and identity in Jesus through lessons, gospel-packed music, powerful testimonies, assemblies and resources.

IN PRISONS...

Our creative mission also sees us heading into prisons and young offenders' institutes across the globe, working with some of society's most broken people. Having fallen on hard times and caught up in lives of crime, many have hit rock-bottom and need to hear about the hope Jesus offers them. Day in, day out, our Message in Prisons teams go into prisons sharing the good news of Jesus in word and deed.

This isn't just through chapel services and Bible study groups. Peacemaker courses teach individuals skills to help them resolve conflict and manage their emotions; mentoring programmes equip them for life outside of prison, and music classes provide a way that relationships can be built with prisoners. God is moving in prisons and lives are being transformed forever.

Our work doesn't stop at the prison gates – we continue working with ex-offenders so that they can break free of the cycle of offending for good and grow in their relationship with Jesus. Through our Christ-centred enterprises we provide people with

'I've been through a lot in my life, and there have been times I've felt the only option is to give up. Your message that 'there is hope' showed me that there is something more. I always thought that there was no God, but this has completely changed.'

'I was so desperate for love that I used to look for it in all the wrong places. Before I knew it I was caught up in drugs, crime and self-harm. The day I met Jesus everything changed. I knew I was loved unconditionally. My job at the Message Enterprise Centre has helped me rebuild my life, grow in my faith and find a purpose for the first time in my life.'

full-time jobs and training, as well as the safe, local accommodation and support they need. Discipleship is at the heart of everything we do, helping each of our team members deepen their faith and love for God.

IN COMMUNITIES...

The gospel is for everyone, and our heart burns for the poor.

Life in the poorest communities is often tough and these are places that often feel unloved and forgotten. We want people that call these places home to know how loved they are, so our Eden teams do life with them for the long term. Partnering with local churches, our Eden teams move into communities across the globe named as the 10% most deprived. Here they build relationships, support their neighbours and share the good news of Jesus. The fruit is lasting transformation – levels of crime and antisocial behaviour drop, people discover Jesus, and urban heroes are raised up.

One way we can show people who Jesus is, is by helping keep them fed. The pandemic and the cost of living increase this created has seen food poverty across the UK soar, so The Message Trust, in partnership with local churches, has stepped up to help make sure no family goes hungry. Bridging the gap between foodbanks and supermarkets, Community Groceries give families access to affordable food as well as wrap-around support, too.

EQUIPPING AND TRAINING...

Young people passionate about sharing the gospel can come and spend a year here with us at The Message being trained and equipped to tell people about Jesus. From day one at Message

School of Evangelism, they not only get taught about evangelism but get to put what they've heard into action with the least, the last and lost. As the students step out in mission, they seize every opportunity to see communities around them changed for good.

We're also desperate to make sure evangelists of all ages are equipped to share the good news of Jesus. Back in 2015, Andy Hawthorne started meeting with a group of 12 others passionate about telling Jesus. As they encouraged, equipped and empowered each other in their evangelism, they felt God say that he wanted them to use this model to build up and envision evangelists across the globe.

Today, Advance Groups are running in over 80 nations across the globe. Through small group mentoring, these groups help Jesus followers share his love with the world around them through their lips and in their lives.

ALL IN PARTNERSHIP...

Our heart is to see every decision to follow Jesus grow into lifelong discipleship, which is why we do everything in partnership with local churches who are 'boots on the ground' in their communities.

As Message teams share the gospel, the local church we're working with to make the mission happen is right there alongside us ready to start building a long-term relationship – getting them plugged into discipleship courses, youth groups or church activities straight away.

It's partnership like this that made it possible for ourselves, 300 churches and the Luis Palau Association to put on Festival

'Because of the Community Grocery, not only have my food needs been met but I've found Jesus and have so much more joy now!'

'All glory to God for an unforgettable party where the church blessed the city, the city blessed the church, and heaven blessed earth!'

Festival Manchester 2022, Wythenshawe Park

THE MESSAGE TRUST

Manchester 2022 – the biggest Christian mission in a generation – that saw over 100,000 people hear the gospel and thousands respond to it.

And it's a model that works. Churches grow, lives are changed, and burning hearts to tell others about Jesus are ignited.

- Will you pray for us?
- Could you join an Eden team?
- Or our Message Academy Evangelists' Training School?
- Would you like to launch an Advance group?

To make all this happen, we need an ever-growing number of people standing with us financially, either with a one-off gift, or even better, monthly by Direct Debit.

If you can help, go to **message.org.uk/donate**

Let's do this together!